Coigners, and Sir Christopher, the twentieth generation, adopted the orthography of Conyers. In Navarre, in the sixteenth century, the residence of a family of this name was known as the Château de Coigniers. Those bearing the name were Huguenots, or French Protestants. In the massacre of St. Bartholomew's day, in 1572, many of this family fell victims to the rage of the Papists, and Pierre Coigners, who was attached to the court of Henry IV of France, having witnessed the assassination of his kinsman, Admiral Coligny, and, fearful of his own safety, escaped with his wife and two infants to England, and settled in the county of Essex, where his son married a lady of considerable possessions in that and an adjoining county. It was Ralph, a son of this marriage, who was created a baronet by King Charles II.

"In England the name was naturally changed to Conyers, corresponding with the English pronunciation, and members of the family still spell the name in this manner, while others, in the change of a single letter, have taken the name of Convers. From these emigrations to England is descended the Converse family of this country. The name was spelled Convers for several generations after the emigration to New England. The coat-of-arms of Coigniers, Conyers, and Convers is essentially the same, which sustains the tradition that all are of a common origin."

An engraving, taken from an illustration furnished by the Rev. J. K. Converse, of Burlington, Vermont, presents the emblems of heraldry which, for many generations, have been associated with the family name, and is read as follows: *Arms.* Argent upon Bend Sable between two Maunches Azure, Trefoils. On Crest an Arm in Armor out of a Mural Crown Gold.

The term argent represents that the shield is white, or of silver color, and sable that the bend, or belt, is black; the bend is a scarf of honor for courage in battle; the trefoils

are emblems of the Trinity, and were bestowed for service in the maintenance of the church; the maunches, or empty sleeves, were added to the arms of those who had been celebrated ·in the councils of sovereigns; the mural crown represents a battlement, and was bestowed on those who first mounted the walls and there lodged a standard; and the motto: *In Deo Solo Confido*, "In God alone I· trust."

From this Huguenot, and by adoption English, family came Edward Converse, one of Winthrop's famous company of emigrants, who arrived in New England in 1630. A man of more than usual enterprise, we find him, from the very outset, ever restlessly pushing forward some new work. In less than a year after settling in Charlestown, he established a ferry, the first between Charlestown and Boston. By order of the court, June 14, 1631, he was authorized, under certain rules and regulations, to manage this enterprise, and for several years it was a leading part of his business. In Winthrop's History of New England, we find the following account, given also in substance in Frothingham's History of Charlestown: —

"The governor and treasurer, by order of the General Court, did demise to Edward Converse the ferry between Boston and Charlestown, to have the sole transporting of passengers and cattle from one side to the other, for three years from the first day of the next month, for the yearly rent of forty pounds to be paid quarterly to the treasurer: Provided that he see it be well attended and furnished with sufficient boats, and that so soon as may be in the next spring he set up a convenient house on Boston side, and keep a boat there, as need shall require, and he is allowed to take his wonted fees, namely, 2*d.* for a single person, and 1*d.* apiece if there be more than one, as well on lecture days as at other times; and for every horse and cow with the man that goeth with them, 6*d.*, and for a goat 1*d.*, and for a swine 2*d.*; and if any shall desire to pass before it is light in the

morning, or if it is after dark in the evening, he may take recompense answerable to the season and his pains and hazard, so it be not excessive."

This lease was given in 1631, and November 9, 1637, it was renewed for three years, Mr. Converse agreeing to pay each year forty pounds into the colonial treasury. This ferry, which crossed the river where now the Charlestown bridge crosses it, was called the "Great Ferry," to distinguish it from another which Thomas Williams had "set up," a short time before its establishment, between Charlestown and Winnisimmet.

Meanwhile Edward Converse was made, during the first year of engagement with the ferry (1631), a freeman of the Colony, and subsequently served the town of Charlestown on the board of selectmen from 1635 until his removal to his new home in the wilderness, which afterward became Woburn. This removal appropriately introduces his connection with the enterprise of founding the new town. It is hardly too much to say that he was on every committee and had a part in every movement that had this new settlement in view. He was one of the small company, who, in September, 1640, went from Charlestown to search the unexplored land to the northward, and experienced an almost miraculous escape from death in a terrific night-storm by the fall of a large tree under which they had laid themselves down for the night. He was one of a committee of thirteen chosen by the town of Charlestown, November 4, 1640, "to sett the bounds betwixt Charlestown and the Village, and to appoint the place for the village." His name stands first in a list of seven men chosen by the church in Charlestown, November 5, 1640, the day after the appointment of the town committee of thirteen, as commissioners for "erecting a church and town" and "for the carr[y]ing on the affaires of this new Town." Six of these seven commissioners were on the town committee of thirteen, and to these six men,

with Edward Converse at the head, was due the success of
the enterprise they had in view. At their first meeting,
held December 18, 1640, thirty-two men were found ready
to affix their names to the Town Orders for Woburn, upon
which they had agreed, the name of Edward Converse being
second in the list. Meanwhile the fears of the church at
Charlestown had been aroused by the zeal and energies of
this handful of men, lest the town should be depopulated.
But they went steadily forward, and the church at length
yielded, Converse and his associates being accorded, December 22, full power to go on with their work. As ever,
Converse seems to have outstripped all others in his zeal,
and to have erected a house in the territory of the proposed
town, previous to January 4, 1641, for, under this date, a
meeting was held at his house, according to Johnson's
Wonder-Working Providence, in which many persons were
admitted to "set down their dwellings in this town, yet
being shallow of brains, fell ofe (off) afterwards." It is
possible, as some writers have suggested, that the meeting
was held at his house in Charlestown, and the words "in
this town" refer simply to what was "this town" when
Johnson wrote. But early in the next month, February 10,
1641, the same writer tells us, as others also do, that the
first bridge was laid over the "Abersonce," elsewhere and
generally called the Abajona,[1] River, "over against Edward
Converse's *house*," and called "Could [or Cold] Bridge."
This record also seems to assume that the house was there
when the bridge was built, though, of course, the reference
to it may possibly, but not naturally, be in anticipation of
its actual erection. Mr. Champney, in his contribution to
the History of Middlesex County, vol. ii, p. 526, after
saying that the bridge was built in February, 1641, adds:
"and the first dwelling-house was erected over against *it*,"
that is, the bridge. This is doubtless correct, so far as the

[1] This name is written Aberjonah, Abarjona, and Abajona by different writers,—the
latter the most frequently in modern usage. — ED.

location of the house was concerned, but it exactly reverses
the statements of the records and of the historian, which
affirm that the bridge was built "over against the house";
the statement of the former implying that the bridge was
built first, and that of the latter, that the house was built
first. Whatever may have been the exact date of the erection of the house, there seems to be no doubt that it was
the first dwelling-house erected in Woburn: that of John
Mousall being built but a little later on "Hilly Way." In
the words of the quaint old historian and poet, Johnson,
referring to these men: —

> "Too [two] nurses less undaunted then [than] the rest,
> ffirst howses ffinish."

The *location* of the Converse house involves difficulties
and differences that seem to demand a notice more extended
than can well be given here; and it is therefore thought
best, on the whole, to defer a consideration of it to an
appendix, where it will appear in connection with "The
description of Edward Converse's possessions in 1638, and
his will in 1659."

The historical facts of the first house and the first bridge,
and probably also the first mill, in Woburn, so intimately
associated with Edward Converse's enterprise, appropriately
introduce us to the part he acted in the organization and
affairs of the new town.

We have already noticed that his name is at the head of
the seven commissioners appointed to superintend the general business of settling the town, which issued in securing
the act of incorporation in 1642. His connection with the
work of gathering the church previous to October 6 of that
year (the date of the incorporation), we pass for the present,
in order to notice more consecutively his secular life and
activities. To the persistent agency of Edward Converse,
more than to any other one man, the success of the seven

commissioners seems to have been due. And when
"Charlestown Village" was finally called "Woobourne,"
by the act of the General Court, and recognized as the twentieth town in the Massachusetts Colony, we can easily
imagine that the satisfaction and joy of no other man
equaled those of this ever-restless worker.

Why the newly incorporated municipality did not immediately so far organize as to choose the appropriate officers
for administering its affairs is at present wholly a matter of
conjecture. The records mention a general meeting as early
as November 9, 1643, in which some minor and comparatively
unimportant matters of business were transacted, but there
is no hint of a regular organization till April 13, 1644, about
eighteen months after the incorporation. On that day, the
freemen of the town made choice of the first board of selectmen, consisting of Edward Johnson, Edward Converse, John
Mousall, William Learned, Ezekiel Richardson, Samuel
Richardson, and James Thompson — seven good and honest
men. The name of Edward Converse stands second on this
board, as given in the Woburn records. From this time
onward until his death, he appeared, as ever before, to have
been a foremost man in all public business. On March 3,
1649, he was one of four of the selectmen appointed to
negotiate with the town of Charlestown the matter of the
disputed boundary between the two towns. He was also,
year after year, one of a board of commissioners for the trial
of "small causes." In 1660 he was deputy to the General
Court. And for nineteen years, from 1644 till 1663, when
he died, he was annually chosen a member of the board of
selectmen.

We come now to a consideration of Edward Converse, in
his *religious character and life.*

In the very outset of his career as a citizen of Charlestown, we find his name in the list of subscribers to the First
Church covenant of that town (August 27, 1630), the first

name being that of Governor Winthrop. When this original First Church was removed, three months afterward, to Boston, though his relation to it for some time remained as before, he did not, like Winthrop and many others, remove his family across the river. Accordingly, when the present First Church of Charlestown was organized (November 2, 1632), he and others, having obtained letters of dismission from the church in Boston, united with those who had not been members of that church in the new organization. As a member of that church, he was ever prominent; and was one of the seven members of it who were commissioned to effect, in the name of the mother church, as also in the presence and with the consent of the appointed representative of the Colony, the outward organization of the church in Woburn. This organization was effected August 24, 1642, and on the second day of the following December Thomas Carter was ordained and installed pastor. It is highly probable, though not definitely ascertained, that, of the two men who laid their hands on the young candidate's head and formally ordained him to the work of the ministry, instead of delegating the power to the messengers of the churches, Edward Converse was one. It is certain that he was one of the first two deacons of the church, and remained in office till his death.

From all that has been ascertained respecting the religious character of Edward Converse, we readily infer that he was a man of strongly marked idiosyncrasies. Prompt, clear-headed, devout, conscientious, outspoken, and unflinching, and yet prudent, self-contained, and uniform, are the adjectives that best describe his whole career. A single curious incident, mentioned by Johnson in his *Wonder-Working Providence*, well illustrates a trait which often seems to manifest itself. It occurred more than twenty years after his removal from Charlestown to Woburn, and only about three months before his death. "In May, 1663, Isaac Cole, constable, and Edward Converse, one of Capt. Johnson's asso-

ciates in the Board of Selectmen at Woburn, were arraigned; the former for refusing to take and publish the King's letter, and the latter for having spoken of it as Popery. The Court, after a hearing, discharged Converse, on the ground that his language did not reflect on his Majesty's letter." This account assumes that Converse did speak of the king's letter as popery, but in language so carefully guarded that even papal servants of the king could not easily make out a case against him.

But though the good old father of the town came forth from his arrest by the officers of the king unscathed and apparently untroubled, there was one passage in his busy life as a citizen which seems to have seriously disturbed him and which resulted in an arbitration between him and one of his neighbors. The erection and operation of his mill on the Abajona River so overflowed the adjacent meadow of Robert Hale as to be an insuperable obstacle in the way of the latter's improvement of his own land. This naturally led to complaint and difficulty. But at length an honorable arbitration seems to have happily ended the controversy in a very fair and Christian way. The paper which gives the terms of the adjustment is dated 1649, and is given in the paper of Mr. A. E. Whitney, which follows this.

This paper is signed by John Mousall, John Wright, Edward Johnson, Miles Nutt, Samuel Richardson, and James Thompson. These six men were all friends of Converse, and at this time associated with him on the board of selectmen. It does not appear that they were not also the friends of Hale. They seem, therefore, to have been, in all respects, very suitable men to act as arbitrators in this case, and their decision seems to have given entire satisfaction to the differing parties.

Of. Edward Converse in his domestic relations more might be said than our present limits would justify. We

have not the full name of his first wife, nor the date of his
first marriage. We only know that her name was Sarah,
and that they were married several years before their
embarkation from England for the New World. Of their
four children, three were born in England: Josiah about
1618, James about 1620, and Mary probably about 1622:
their ages being respectively twelve, ten, and eight years,
when the family came to Charlestown. The fourth child,
Samuel, was born in Charlestown, March 12, 1638. Each of
the three sons had an honorable history worthy of separate
notice. The sad death of Samuel, in 1669, by an accident
in the old Converse Mill, has been well described in a valuable paper lately read by Mr. A. E. Whitney before the
Winchester Historical and Genealogical Society. The
daughter Mary married, December 19, 1643, Simon Thompson, the second son of James Thompson, of the North
Village in Woburn, and, like Edward Converse, one of
the first settlers of the town and one of the first board of
selectmen. Of the two sons and four daughters of Simon
and Mary (Converse) Thompson only two, one son and one
daughter, are known to have lived to reach maturity. The
son, a young man in his twentieth year, and named James
for his grandfather, was in the mill with his uncle Samuel
when the fatal accident to the latter occurred. His mother,
Mary Converse, having been left a widow in 1658, married,
in 1659, John Sheldon, of Billerica. There she had another
son, John Sheldon, Jr., who, at the time of his death, in
1724, was a deacon of the church in that place. Meanwhile
her father, Deacon Edward Converse, lost his wife, January
14, 1662, and, in nine months after her death, and in less
than a year before his own death, which occurred August 10,
1663, he married, September 9, 1662, Joanna Sprague, the
widow of Ralph Sprague, of Charlestown. For more convenient reference, the family record, gathered from various
sources, is given in the following condensed form : —

Edward Converse, b. England, January 30, 1590; d. August 10, 1663, aged seventy-three years. m. Sarah ——. Children: —

1. Josiah, b. England, 1618 (deacon); d. February 3, 1690, aged seventy-two years. m. Esther, daughter of Richard Champney, of Cambridge, March 26, 1651.
2. James, b. England, 1620 (lieutenant); d. May 10, 1715, aged ninety-five years. m. Anna, daughter of Robert Long, of Charlestown, October 24, 1643.
3. Mary, b. England, 1622; d. ——. m. Simon Thompson, January 19, 1643. m. 2d, John Sheldon, February 1, 1659.
4. Samuel, b. Charlestown, March 12, 1637; d. February 20, 1669, aged thirty-one years. m. Judith, dau. Rev. Thomas Carter, June 8, 1660.

Edward Converse, m., 2d, Joanna, widow of Ralph Sprague, of Charlestown, September 9, 1662.

NOTE.— The more extended genealogy of the family of Edward Converse is reserved for a future number of *The Record.*   G. C.

APPENDIX.

The following account of the possessions of Edward Converse, in 1638, is taken from the Third Report of Commissioners of the City of Boston and Charlestown Land Records : —

" The Possession of Edward Converse within Charltowne Limites.

" 1. One roode of grownde by estimation, more or lesse, scituate in the middle row, butting north west and south west upon the market place, south east upon the marsh towards the harbour, bounded on the north east by Capt. Sedgewick, with a dwelling-house, store-house, and other aptinances.

" 2. Ffive acres of earable land by estimation, more or lesse, scituate in the east feilde butting south-west upon the long way; north east upon Will Bates, bounded on the north west by George Bunker, and on the south east by Mr. Symmes, Capt. Sedgewick, and Rice Cole.

" 3. One acre and haulfe of earable land by estimation,

more or lesse, scituate in the east feilde, butting south west upon the back streete, northeast upon Will Johnson, bounded on the southeast by Will Dade, and upon the northwest by Sam. Carter.

"4. Three acres of meadow by estimation, more or lesse, scituate in the south meaddowes, butting north west toeards the streete way, south-east upon a creeke, bounded on the south-west by Mr. Simmes, and on the north east by Ra. Sprague.

"5. One acre of meadow by estimation, more or less, scituate in the south meade.

"6. Comons for milch cowes ffive and a quarter.

"7. Two acress of meaddow by estimation, more or less, scituate and being in the line Feilde, with a p'cell of upland adioining on the west side of it, bounded on the west by the high-way; on the east by Winstamies river, on the south by Mr. Simmes, and on the north by George Bunker.

"8. Eight acres of erable land by estimation, more or less, scituate in the line-Feilde, butting east upon the highway; west upon Rob. Long, bounded on the south by Mr. Simmes, and on the northe by Daniell Shepeardson and Will Brakenbury.

"9. Three acres of meaddow by estimation, more or lesse, lying on the north of mount P'spect, bounded on the west by the river, on the east by the Comon, on the South by Ezecheall Richardson, and on the northe by Tho. Lynde.

"10. Ffive acres of woodland, more or lesse, scituate in Mistick Feilde, butting west and south upon the drift way, east upon the landway, bounded on the north by George Hutchinson.

"11. Thirtie and ffive acres of woodland, more or less, scituate in Mistick Feilde, butting south west upon the reserved land, north east upon Will Brakenbury, James Pemberton, and Peter Garland, bounded on the north west by Tho. Moulton, and on the south east by John Martin.

"12. Eightie acres of land by estimation, more or lesse, scituate in Waterfeilde, bounded on the east by the river, on the north west by Eze. Richardson, Rob. Rand, Tho. Moulton, and John Crow ; on the north west [1] by Tho. Moulton, John Martin, and Mr. Simmes.

"13. Ffive acres of Woodland, more or lesse, scituate in Mistick Feilde, butting south west upon George Bunker, north east upon Ed. Mellowes, bounded on the north west by George Whiteland, and on the south west by John Tedd."

The will of Edward Converse, dated August, 1659, is as follows : —

"In the name of God, Amen, I, Edward Convers, of Woburne, in the Coun. of Midd. in the Massachusetts Collony in New England, being in p-fect memory though weake of Body, do make this my last will and testamt, to dispose of my lands, goods and chattles, that the Lord hath lent unto mee, dureing my naturall life, which my Will is shall be disposed of in mannr as followeth.

"Imp. I give and bequeath unto my beloved wife Sarah Convers ten pounds pr. a year, to be payd unto Her from yeare to yeare during her *naturall* life, that is to say, five pounds a yeare out of my sonne Josias Convers his house, and ye other five pounds a year out of the Mill. Also my will is that my wife shall have such roomes to live in dureing her life in the house that I now live in, as She shall make choyce of for Her use, and one of the gardens before the house, which she shall make choyce of for her use, and ten of the apple trees in the old orchard dureing her life which she shall make choyce of. Also my will is that my wife shall have a fourth part of all my moveable goods and chattels when my debts and legacyes and my funall be discharged. Also I give unto my sonne, Josias Convers, the

[1] Apparently an error either in the transcription or type. Probably it should be *northeast.* The *northwest* boundary precedes.

House wherein He now liveth and the barnes and outhouses
and the orchard before the house, with the yards and other
appurtenances to the same belonging, and the land that lyeth
in the great field, and all that meadow that lyeth in the west
side of the brooke in bucke meadow. My Will is that my
sonne Josias shall enjoy all these houses and lands, with other
the appurtenances above specified, for Him and his heyres
lawfully begotten of his body, and for want thereof, to my
sonne James Converse, his sonne Edward Convers, and to his
Heyres lawfully begotten of his body, and for want thereof
my Will is that it shall be divided between the rest of my
sonne James his children equally, or to the next Heyre
according to law, and for the field called the sheep-pasture, I
give it to my to sonnes Josiah and Samuel together with my
mill and mill house and the appurtenances to them belonging, to be possessed by the longest liver and his Heyres.
Also I give to my sonne Samuel Convers my house wherein
I now dwell and all the land lying behind the house to the
brow of ye Hill northward, and all the land that is plowable
lying on the north side of the blind bridge, together with
all the meadow that lyeth adjoyning to the said land and all
that p'cell of land that lyeth on the east side of the rode,
next to the mill pond betweene the aforesaid blynd Bridge,
and my dwelling house. Also I give to my sonne Samuel
all ye meadow land yt lyeth on ye east side of the river in
Bucke meadow, and my English pasture that is fenced in on
the other side the mill river, and my will is that for all the
rest of ye land that is not plowable lying on the north side
of blind Bridge, together with all the rest of my pasture
lands, shall be equally divided between my three sonnes,
Josiah, James, and Samuel, only reserveing the timber that
is upon the said pasture lands from my sonne James, who
shall have no part therein, but it shall be injoyed by my
other to sonnes Josiah and Samuel and their Heyres. Also
my will is that if my sonne Samuel shall dy without Heyres

lawfully begotten of his body, that the estate that I have given to Him shall be divided between ye children of my daughter Mary Thompson. Also I give to my sonne James Convers the sume of thirty pounds and I give to my daughter Mary Sheldon the sume of twenty marks. And I give to my kinsman Allin Convers the sume of ten pounds, and I give to my kinswoman Sarah Smith the sume of five pounds. Also I give to my kinsman John Parker the sume of forty shillings, and for these legacyes my will is that they shall be paid within three years after my decease as my Executors shall see meete and are able to pay the same. and for all that land that lyeth comon between the houses my will is that it shall ly comon for perpetuity, and for all my moveable goodes and chattels that remaineth of what is given to my wife, I give to thirds of the same to my sonne Josiah and the other third to my sonne Samuel. and for the legacyes that I have given my will is that they shall be payd in Corne and cattle, or either of them. Also my will is that my sonne Josiah and my sonne Samuel shall be my sole executors. Also my will is that my sonne James Convers and my kinsman Allin Convers, and my kinsman John Parker shall be the overseers of this my Will. My will also is that all my moveable goods shall be apprised distinctly.

"Signed and subscribed the —— day of August, 1659.

"EDWARD CONVERS."
[And a seal.]

In the presence of us,

ALLIN CONVERS,
JNO. PARKER.

" My Will is that my sonne Josiah shall have the meadow that is fenced in on the other side of the mill brook, lying next unto my sonne James his meadow for Him and his Heyres, as the rest of the lands within expressed.

"Cambridge 7, 8th, 1663. At the Coun Court then sitting at Cambridge, Allin Convers and John Parker

appearing in Court, do on their oath given them say that Edward Convers deced being of a disposeing mind, they saw Him signe, seale and publish this instrumet as his last Will and testament, and that they know of no other.

"Entred and Recorded, 7, 8th, 1663.

"THOMAS DANFORTH, *Record.*"

In immediate connection with the foregoing documents, we come at length to a consideration of Edward Converse's house. The writer approaches this part of our general subject with some hesitancy, not because he has no settled opinion of his own to express, but because he is aware that his opinion is not accordant with that of some others whose views he is both bound and inclined to respect. For more than sixty years, he has been accustomed to hear the oldest people in Woburn say that the house of Edward Converse stood on the east side of the road and between the road and the river, on or very near the site of the house of the late Deacon Benjamin F. Thompson. And till recently, he never knew that any man entertained the opinion that it stood on the west side of the road near the house of the late .S. S. Richardson. Least of all was he prepared, with the record of Converse's possessions and a copy of his will before him, to hear the statement that Converse *never owned any land on the east side of the road.*

As the writer can express only his own views and give his reasons for them, he has no alternative but to do so and leave it to others to exercise the same liberty.

The only article of the thirteen describing the possessions of Edward Converse within Charlestown limits in 1638, which is understood to have any reference to lands in the territory that, four years later, became that part of Woburn now included in Winchester, is the twelfth. This describes eighty acres, situated in Waterfielde. Waterfielde is believed to be the region, or rather includes the region, lying west

of the Abajona River at Winchester, extending some distance
northerly, and farther westerly, including the vicinity of
Horn Pond and perhaps reaching still farther west. Whatever may have been the extent of these lands, it is clear that
the river, and not the road, was the eastern boundary of that
part of them owned by Converse.

Further, in his will, twenty-one years later, Edward
Converse not only bequeathed to his son Samuel property
lying on "the east side of the rode," but also meadow-land
that lay on the "East side of the *river*," thus revealing the
fact that, during the intervening years between the dates
of these two papers, he had acquired considerable land on
the other side of that well-known stream. Keeping these
important items in distinct view, the writer would suggest
the following reasons for his belief that the original Converse
house stood on the site above suggested : —

1. There is nothing in the "Possessions" that *precludes*
the conclusion that the Converse house was on the east side
of the road. On the contrary, Edward Converse, even
before he built it, owned all the land between the road and
the river from the bridge for some distance northerly.

2. His will clearly implies that he not only still owned
this land in 1659,-when he gave it away, but had acquired
a considerable tract of other land on the east side of the
river.

3. The natural implication of the oft-recurring words
"over against," in the various notices of the house and mill
and the adjacent bridge, is that the house and mill were on
opposite sides, and not on the same side, of the road. It
may safely be presumed that, in a vast majority of instances,
if not in all, in which this familiar form of words is
employed, it implies this. (See Webster and Worcester
on the words "over" and "against.")

4. The bequests of the will in the light of subsequent
facts.

It will be noticed that the father gives the house in which he himself lived, with certain qualifications, to his son Samuel, who was to have the special care of the mill. He also gives him "all the land lying *behind* the house to the brow of the Hill *northward*," etc. The land "behind" a house on the opposite side of the road from, that of the traditional site could not, it does not seem, extend to the brow of a hill "northward." It would be southward indefinitely and no "hill." On the contrary, the land in the rear of, and northerly from, the traditional site does extend to higher ground at no very great distance. And this house, thus given to Samuel, was that one of several houses which, as we should expect in the home of the miller, was nearest to the mill. Then, as Samuel did not long survive his father to occupy it, it seems reasonable that James, to whom, unlike both the other sons, his father had *given no house*, should succeed to the occupancy of the homestead. If this be so, it explains the fact, otherwise not accounted for, that in subsequent years we find James there, as is assumed by Mr. Sewall in his History of Woburn (pp. 176, 177), and in the familiar story of the Honorable Judge. Sewall stopping there on his journey and "discoursing" him under the far-famed shady elm in 1702.

It hardly need be added that there is no lack of evidence that this venerable and well-remembered tree was, like old ancestral shade-trees generally, on the same side of the road with, and immediately in front of, the house. If the old tradition concerning the ancient house, which many still remember, is reliable, this tree was certainly so located as to overshadow it; as it did also, till cut down (about 1841), the house of Deacon B. F. Thompson, on or very near the same spot.

5. The traditions and early impressions of the oldest people of both the past and the present time.

It has already been stated that the writer, who cannot

remember the day when he was not curious to know and treasure up all such stories of the olden time, never till of late heard any other tradition than the one to which he still adheres. He distinctly remembers hearing often in his childhood days this account of the old house, then occupied by Abel Richardson.

George R. Baldwin, Esq., now in his eighty-eighth year, testifies that, when a boy, he attended a school in Medford, and was continually passing the spot to and from that place, and then, as now, believed the house to be that of Edward Converse.

The writer recently met Sherman Converse, Esq., of Woburn, now seventy-five years old, a lineal descendant of Edward Converse, and, before stating his object, asked him if he remembered any family tradition in regard to the site of the first Converse house. Very promptly he replied: "Yes; when I was a boy, my father [1] carried me to the old house, then occupied by Abel Richardson, and told me *that* was the house of his ancestor, Edward Converse."

A few days later, on meeting Judge Parker L. Converse, a son of Luther Converse, and also a descendant of Edward, the writer proposed a similar question and received for answer a reiteration of the same family tradition; he adding, and repeating with emphasis: "I *know* that my father used to say it was *there.*"

6. The former condition of the land adjacent to the river on the west, or at this locality the southwest, side of the road.

Within the memory of some persons now living, a wet boggy marsh, sometimes overflowed, extended from the river up beyond the site of S. S. Richardson's house. The writer well remembers this low and wet region, and has been told that it was not till after a very large amount of gravel and soil from a neighboring hill had been carted there, that it

---

[1] The late Joshua Converse, who lived to be more than one hundred years of age.

was at all suitable for the sites of the dwellings now there. It might have been utilized for a mill or a barn, and indeed there is reason to believe that one of the barns of Edward Converse actually stood there, with a cellar under a part of it, against whose walls there was an occasional overflow of water. But it could not have been suitable for a human habitation.

This reason for rejecting the supposition that the Converse house stood on this side of the road introduces another, and the last, which will be here given.

7. The singularly shrewd sagacity of the man.

No trait in the character of Edward Converse stands out in the record of his whole career with more prominence than that of his quick good sense: his ability to see at a glance the best things, and to seize upon the most promising opportunities for accomplishing a desirable object. The writer of this paper has all along been so impressed, in his investigation, with this trait of *the man*, that it seems to him exceedingly improbable, if not impossible, that *such an owner of the land on both sides of the road* would reject the more elevated, and every way very eligible, location behind the great elm on the east side, and choose instead the wet boggy lowland on the opposite side, of the road.

L. THOMPSON.

THE OLD HOME OF EDWARD CONVERSE.

WOBURN, August 24, 1885.

ABIJAH THOMPSON, ESQ.

Dear Sir, — In an interview with an aunt of mine, Miss Lydia Converse, who is a direct descendant of Deacon Edward Converse, one of the principal founders of the town, and also one of the first two deacons of the First Church of Woburn, she, without any hesitation, says that the old house which

formerly stood on the lot of land now occupied by the house built by your father, the late Deacon Benjamin F. Thompson, on the easterly side of Main Street, and known by the older inhabitants as the Abel Richardson house, was built, owned, and occupied by Deacon Edward Converse, and that he continued to occupy the premises during his life. She states furthermore that this was the first house built within the limits of the town, the second being that of Deacon John Mousall, and was located on what is now Montvale Avenue, on or near lot of land now owned and occupied by Mrs. George Reed, in Woburn Centre. Deacon Mousall and Deacon Converse were the first two deacons of the First Church of Woburn, and were intimately associated in the affairs of both town and church.

Yours, etc.
ALVAH S. WOOD.

The above statement is in accordance with my knowledge and belief.

LYDIA CONVERSE.

THE MYSTERIOUS CELLARS.

IN 1857 Joel F. Hanson bought of Lorenzo Dupee the farm then known as the George Wyman place, situated on Cambridge Street, nearly opposite to the place then called the Luke Reade farm.

At this time, in the north corner of his farm, and near the shore of Winter Pond, Mr. Hanson found the remains of two cellars — one supposed to have been the site of a house, the other that of a barn. At a little distance from the former was a hedge of a kind of shrub often used in England for that purpose, but not a native of this country; on the other side of this hedge-row was an old well, nearly filled with stones and rubbish.

The bricks found in these ruined cellars were English face-bricks. Near the house cellar stood two large elm-trees, the grass beneath them being soft, fine, and long, — like wood-grass, — as if undisturbed for many years.

No information could be gathered as to " what manner of man " once lived there. The oldest person then living in that neighborhood did not remember any buildings on these cellars, nor had heard from any source of buildings having been there. It had been observed that the old well was as well stoned as any ever seen, and it was evident that the people living there must have been very early settlers, bringing from their English home the bricks and the favorite homestead shrubbery; these, with the cellars themselves, being all that had survived the ravages of time.

Mr. Hanson, for several years, kept these relics undisturbed; but finally, wishing to use the land, cut down the ancient elm-trees and filled the mysterious cellars.

Mrs. STEPHEN S. LANGLEY.

Winchester, March 3, 1885.

The solution of this mystery is to be found in Sewall's History of Woburn, containing the

GENEALOGY OF RICHARD GARDNER.

" *Richard Gardner* came," says the family tradition, " from the county of Surrey, England, and settled first within the bounds of Woburn, having his house *nearly opposite to the mansion of the late Luke Reed, Esq.*, in Woburn West End, about forty rods from the road, where the remains of the cellar and well were discernible in 1857.

" But between 1661 and 1667 he removed to ' Charlestown End,' to the spot where the two maiden ladies, Miss Patience Gardner and her sister, had their habitation."

This, therefore, was the " manner of man " who selected that beautiful site on the shore of Winter Pond, and the

following genealogical table will remind many Winchester families of their own connection with Mrs. Langley's tale of "The Mysterious Cellars."

The reason for the abandonment of the premises thus admirably selected, and both tastefully and expensively improved, is not given in any record at present within our reach, and we may conjecture that no reason less than a serious question of title to the land could probably have led to this result.

The " Charlestown End " place, named above, is that now known as the Magee place, near the junction of Church and Cambridge Streets, Winchester. " Gardner's Row " extended from Cooke's, afterward Cutter's, mill, in Arlington, to this Richard Gardner's (Magee) place. And long after the territory of Woburn was set off, what was subsequently West Cambridge (Arlington) continued a part of Charlestown and was called " Charlestown End."

The Misses Gardner, named by Sewall, were descendants of Richard, and were living at the homestead within the recollection of our older citizens.

The house next south on Cambridge Street was built by Edward Gardner, and subsequently purchased by John Swan, — father of the present occupant. Mr. Samuel Gardner owned and occupied, during his life, the house upon the west side of the same street, next below Mr. Butters, which house, in recent times, was purchased by the late D. N. Skillings, and was afterward destroyed by fire, — the cellar walls still visible. Deacon Henry Gardner lived on High Street, next beyond the Andrews place. These relics of the Gardner family are known to our older citizens. — ED.

NOTE.— In 1652 the town made Increase Nowell the grant of "all that part of lands which Squa Sachem gave formerly unto him, the which he had given to the town, which lies on the south side of his lot next Woburn." This tract of land was sold in 1636, by Mr. Nowell's heirs, to Thomas Broughton, who sold it in 1639 to Richard Gardner. The descendants of the latter have lived on it to the present day (1845). It is known as " Gardner's Row." — *Frothingham's Charlestown, p. 147.*

I. Richard Gardner married Anna Blanchard, of Acton (Savage says, of Charlestown, widow of Thomas, of Mystic Side, or Malden), October 18, 1651, by whom he had: —

1. John, b. August 14, 1652. (Woburn Record Births.)
2. Anna, b. January 17, 1654–5. Died before her father. (Woburn Record Births.)
3. Benjamin, b. December 26, 1656. Died before his father. (Woburn Record Births.)
4. Henry, b. February 12, 1657–8. (Woburn Record Births.)
5. Esther, b. October 15, 1659; m. William Johnson, eldest son of Wm. and Esther. (Woburn Record Births.)
6. Ruth, b. April 1, 1661; m. John Gypson (Gibson?). Woburn Record Births.) Born after removal to Charlestown End.
7. Hannah (Charlestown Records); m. —— Coddington.
8. Abigail (Charlestown Records); m. Jas. Thompson.
9. Rebecca (Charlestown Records); m. Samuel Whittimore, of Cambridge.
10. Mehetabel (Charlestown Records); m. (John) Connet.

Richd. Gardner d. May 29 (al. Mar. 4), 1698, aged about 79. — [Gravestone.]

II. Henry Gardner (4 above); m. Elizabeth ——, by whom he had: —

1. John, b. July 22, 1695.
2. Henry, b. August 2, 1698.
3. Samuel, b. September 10, 1700; d. unmarried, March 3 (al. December 3), 1723.
4. Elizabeth, b. December 25, 1702; m. —— Sawyer.
5. Mary, b. May 28, 1705; "Do. of Charlestown"; m. Zechariah Flagg, Woburn, January 2, 1733.

Henry d. February 20, 1713–14, aged 57, while his son John was in college.

III. John, was graduated Harv. Coll., 1715; ordained at Stow; died, the minister of that town, January 10, 1775, aged 80.

He was the father of the Hon. Henry Gardner, Treas. of Mass. in the time of the Revolution; also of the Rev. Francis Gardner, minister of Leominster. — *Wob. Rec. of Births, etc.*

INSCRIPTIONS FROM THE OLDER BURIAL-GROUNDS IN WOBURN,

RELATING to persons known to have been residents of, or supposed to have been connected with, that part of Woburn now embraced in the town of Winchester. Communicated by William R. Cutter.

From the First, or Oldest, Burying-ground, on Park Street.

CONVERSE.

Memento mori.   Fugit hora.

Here lyes the body of Deacon Josias Conuers aged 72 years deceased the 3 of February 1689–90.[1]

Here lyes ye body of Ann Conuers wife to James Conuers aged 69 years died August the 10 1691.

Edward Conuers son of Edward & Sarah Conuers aged 3 dayes died 28 of Octobr 1691.

Here lyes ye body of Edward Conuers aged 37 years died ye 26 of Iuly 1692.

Timothy Convers son of Josias & Ruth Convers aged 2 mo died September 5 1693.

Ebenezer Convers son of James & Hannah Convers aged about 5 years died Nouember 9th 1693.

Josias Conuers son of Josias & Ruth Conuers aged 3 years died December 30, 1693.

Elizabeth Conuers Daughter of James & Hannah Conuers aged 19 years died Iuly 27 1694.

Here lyes ye body of Esther Convers died November 7th 1703 in the 16 year of her age.

[1] This is the earliest dated stone of any now standing in the yard.

Memento mori.   Fugit hora.

Here lyes buried ye body of Maior Iames Conuers Esqr aged 61 years who departed this life Iuly ye 8th 1706.

Memento mori.   Fugit hora.

Here lyes ye body of Pashence Conver daughter of Maior Iames & Hannah Conver who departed this life Iuly ye 23rd 1707 in ye 21st year of her age.

Here lyes ye body of Sarah Convers who deceased December ye 10th 1713 in ye 25th year of her age.

Memento mori.   Fugit hora.

Here lyes the body of Lieut James Conuers who departed this life May the 10th 1715 in ye 95th year of his age.

The Memory of the Just is Blessed.

Here lyes buried the body of Capt Josiah Convers who departed this life July the 15th 1717 in the 58th year of his age.

The memory of ye Just is Blessed.

Benjamin Converse Son of Capt Robert and Mrs Mary Converse Decd Aug 19th 1729 in ye Eleventh Year of his Age.

Here lyes Buried the Body of Mr Ebenezer Converse,[1] who departed this life Sept ye 6th 1765 in ye 56th Year of His Age.

From the Second Burying-ground, on Montvale Avenue.

Joseph Converse, son & only child of Joseph & Abigail Converse, died August 17, 1803, Æt. 2 years & 5 months.

---

[1] Ebenezer Converse, born November 1, 1708, son of Captain Robert and Mary (Sawyer) Convers (*vide* Sewall's History, 606), and grandson of Major James Convers (see a previous epitaph), was a selectman of Woburn, 1743, 1758, and 1764; and admitted to membership in Woburn First Church, November, 1758 (*vide* Church Manual, p. 10). He married wife, Ruth. His house was in "Carter's Quarter" (South Village), 1742. — *Vide* Sewall's Woburn, 231, etc.

The foregoing are all the stones bearing the Converse name in the first burying-ground.

Erected in memory of Mrs. Hannah Converse, wife of Mr. Jacob Converse, died suddenly, July 13, 1820, Æt. 41.

Therefore, be ye also ready, for in such an hour as ye think not, the Son of Man cometh.

In Memory of Mr. Benjamin Converse,[1] who died March 6th, 1824, in the 73d year of his age.

In Memory of Sarah Converse, who died June 24, 1824, in the 73d year of Her Age.

Erected in Memory of Mrs. Susannah, wife of Dea. Jesse Converse, who died Octr 10, 1825, Æt. 53. [Concludes with four lines of poetry.]

In memory of Dea. Josiah Converse, who died Septr. 8, 1840, in the 82d year of his age.

In memory of Gilman Converse, who died April 14th, 1846, Aged 22 yrs. & 4 mos. [Concludes with four lines of poetry.]

THE OLD CONVERSE MILL.

" MORE servants wait on man
Than he'll take notice of;

For us the winds do blow
The earth doth rest, the Heavens move,
And fountains flow."

GEORGE HERBERT, 1633.

IN the settlement of the early New England villages and towns it was held of the greatest importance to secure a good source of water-supply. It will be remembered that in the early days of Charlestown the want of good water nearly

[1] He lived at Winchester Centre; was son of Ebenezer (epitaph in former yard). Sarah was his widow. She was Sarah Wright, b. July 18, 1748; m. Benjamin Converse, August 6, 1772.

proved fatal to the settlement. "The people grew discontented for want of water, who generally notioned no water good for a town but running springs" (Charlestown Records). The leaders of the colony, including Governor Winthrop, decided, December 6, 1630, to remove from Charlestown to Roxbury and build a town there, but eight days afterward concluded not to do so, as "there was no running water." (Savage's Winthrop, i, 38). Shawmut, Watertown, and Dorchester were settled at this time by people from Charlestown, who were attracted to these places by finding "good waters" there.

After this "dispersion" of the inhabitants of Charlestown, there were left upon the records of the town the names of seventeen who remained, and among them were three who took part in the settlement of that part of Woburn which is now called Winchester: Increase Nowell, Edward Converse, and Ezekiel Richardson.

Edward Converse was the builder and first owner of the "Old Mill" in this town, now known as Whitney's Mill. His house and farm were near this spot. It is very probable that after his experience in Charlestown he appreciated "good waters," and chose the banks of the Abajona.

We shall have the less to say of Edward Converse's life in this paper, as a much fuller paper is being prepared by another member of this Society.

In the earliest records both of Charlestown and Woburn he is prominent as a town and a church officer, as a large taxpayer, and a citizen of great energy and enterprise, as well as leader in some of the most important movements.

The first mention made of him in connection with Woburn or the locality in which we now live, is found in the Records of Charlestown under date of 1635, where we read: "Edward Converse, William Brackenbury, and Mr. Abraham Palmer were desired to go up into the country upon discovery three or four days," for which they were

to be "satisfied at the charge of the town." On subsequent expeditions, made by different parties into this region, then called "Waterfield," Edward Converse was the leader. Those who moved in the matter of settling this town are spoken of thus: "3 of 10 mo.—Full power was given to Edward Conuars and company to go on with the work." The first house erected in Woburn was undoubtedly that of Edward Converse, which was probably close to his mill and near the site of the present Thompson House on Main Street. Here also was erected the first bridge over the "Abersonce," or Abajona, at a point on the river called the "King's Ford," and doubtless near the present bridge. The record by Edward Johnson reads as follows: "10 of 12 mo. —The first bridge was laid over the Abersonce River, over against Edward Conuars house and called Could Bridg."

Another record virtually substantiates the date previous to which the Converse house must have been built. It is the introduction, or prologue, with which Edward Johnson commenced his work as recorder.

"RECORDS FOR THE TOWNE OF WOBURNE.

"ffrom the year 1640: the: 8: day of th: 10 month .
Paulisper Fui.

"In peniles age I, Woburne Towne, began;
Charles Towne first moued the Court my lins to span
To vewe my land place, compild body Reare
Nowell, Sims, Sedgwick, thes my paterons were:
Sum fearing Ile grow great upon these grownds
Poor I wase putt to nurs among the Clownes
Who being taken with such mighty things
As had been work of Noble Qeeins and Kings
Till Babe gan crye and great disturbance make
Nurses Repent they did har undertake
One leaves her quite, another hee doth hie
To foren lands free from the Babys Crye

"A naighbour by, hopeing the Babe wold bee
A pritty Girle, to Rocking har went hee.
Too nurses less undanted then the rest
fflrst houses ffinish, thus the Girle ganc drest.
Its Rare to see how this poore Towne did rise
By weakess means two weake in great ons eys.
And sure it is that mettells cleere exstraction
Had neuer share in this Poore Towns erexiòn
Without which metall and sunn fresh suplys
Patrons conclud she neuer upp wold rise."

This is veritable history, if not poetry, and the characters alluded to are readily understood. The "two nurses" were Edward Converse and John Mousall, whose houses were "finished first," and *prior* to December 8, 1640, the date of this prologue.

We must believe the Converse Mill to have been built very soon after the house. Converse was a man of too much energy to wait a very long time before he set the water at work grinding corn, which was so essential to the people of the new town.[1]

The first legal document we find on record, relating to this mill, recites an agreement or arbitration, under date 20, 12 mo., 1649, — between John Hale and Edward Converse, — before Edward Johnson, as to the flowage of Hale's meadow by Converse's milldam.

This was seven years after the incorporation of the town, and the dam must have been built and the meadow overflowed before the damage complained of could have occurred.

The arbitration reads thus : —

"Upon an Arbitration between Robert Hale and Edward Converse, concerning meadow Land overfllowed by the Mill of the said Edward, It is agreed By us whose names are

---

[1] It is not improbable that in the early work of this mill, as it is said to be the fact in its later history, the water was used only in the winter months, — say from October to April, — and the meadows could thus be cropped during the summer. — ED.

underwritten, that the said Edward Converse shall pay for full satisfaction the sume of seven pounds to the said Robert Hale and this in Current money or in corne or in Cattle at a valluable consideration, provided notwithstanding that If any part of the said meadows be recovered out of the watter it shall be lawfull for the said Robert Hale to repossese the same; paying to the said Edward Converse twentie shillings an Acor for so much as he shall think fitt to make use of againe. And further If the whole shall be recovered, then the said Robt Hale shall Pay Backe Againe the whole sume of seven Pounds, and untell the money be repaid as above Expressed, it shall be used by the said Edward Converse.

"Dated the Twentyeth of the twelfth mo 1649

"The payment of the said sume of seven Pounds to be payd by Edward Converse to Robert hale shall be by the twentyeth of the ninth month next Insueing the date heare of

> "JOHN MOUSALL
> EDWARD JOHNSON
> MILES NUTT
> JOHN WRIGHT
> SAMUEL RICHARDSON [mark] X
> JAMES THOMPSON [mark] T

"This above written Is a true Copy of the Oridginall Writing Compared word for word this: Last day June 1662.   pr me

> "EDWARD BURTT
> "*Recorder.*
> "1662."

We would note, in passing, that Robert Hale lived in Charlestown, and was the ancestor of Nathan Hale, executed by the British in the War of the Revolution as a spy. He owned a meadow lot in "Waterfield," as all the central part of Winchester was then called. This meadow was on the east side of the stream, next to Samuel Richardson's lot of

ninety acres, which latter extended into the "Rock field," as the land along and above our present Highland Avenue was then called.

It may now be asked, How did Edward Converse obtain possession of his land? He obtained it as an inhabitant of Charlestown. The early inhabitants parceled out the lands granted to their respective towns, — sometimes bestowing them for eminent services, at other times dividing them under direction of the selectmen or special committees appointed by the town.[1] And it will be remembered that the earliest immigrants were each entitled to fifty acres of land, by the regulations of the London Company, and also fifty acres for each servant. (Frothingham's History of Charlestown.)

In some or several of the ways named, Converse obtained the thirteen different lots of land accredited to him in the "Charlestown Book of Possessions." In 1638 he is recorded as the owner of these thirteen distinct properties, numbered consecutively in the Records, and No. 12 includes the ground of the present Whitney Mill, as it does also that of the Cutter and the Cowdery, Cobb & Nicholls Mills in Winchester.

The description of this No. 12 is as follows: —

"Eightie Acres of land by estimation, more or lesse, Scituate in Waterfield, bounded east by the river, on the Northwest by Eze. Richardson, Rob. Rand, Tho. Moulton and John Crow: on the Northwest (?) by Tho. Moulton, John Martin and Mr. Simms."

This last boundary is evidently recorded wrong, as the boundaries of Moulton and Symmes "butted Northeast on

[1] "1638. The first month, the 26: day | Abra: Palmer, chosen by the Towne for keepeing the Towne Booke, as also to Record all pprieties of Houses, Lands, Meadow or Pasture, as any Inhabitants of ye Towne are, or shall bee possest of accordg: to an ordr of Court provided in yt behalfe."

"1638.

"On the 28th day of the X month was taken A True Record of all such houses & Lands as are Possessed by the Inhabitants of Charlestown, whethr by purchase, by gift from the Towne, or by allottments as they were devided amongst them by A Joynt Consent aftr the Genll Court had settled theire Bounds," etc. — *Charlestown Records.*

Converse "; which is shown also by the ancient plan of the Symmes farm in the archives of our Society.

If the tender consciences of the present Winchester landholders are troubled with the thought that these lands were stolen from the poor Indian before the town of Charlestown could thus bestow them, the history of Squa Sachem and her deeds of conveyance (as described in *The Record*, by Mr. Symmes, pp. 19–21) will satisfy them, doubtless, that these lands were duly conveyed, and the chain of title was as good as it could well be. And it is interesting to know that it is the opinion of Mr. Frothingham, in his History of Charlestown, that one of Squa Sachem's residences was near Gardner's Row, in West Cambridge, which would bring it near the present residence of Abijah Thompson.

Satisfied that Edward Converse, in common with other ancient landowners in Winchester, had good and sufficient title to his farm and mill privilege, let us consider what business was carried on there in 1640.

It is probable that he used the water-power for no other purpose than to grind corn.

In the old deeds it is invariably called a " corne mill," and no allusion is found to any other uses of the water-power at this point. Indian corn was the principal product of the soil, the principal article of food, and the grinding of it the only business at that date requiring the use of water-power. Power-saws or other machinery for wood or metal were not introduced till long after this date.

But so important was the cornmill that it determined the location and construction of the highways.

" Plain St.," now Cambridge Street, was laid out in 1646 from Woburn to Captain Cook's mill (referred to in Squa Sachem's deed, *The Record*, p. 21), professedly to reach that mill; and " Driver's Lane," now Church Street, leading from the " King's Ford " (near Converse's mill) to Plain

Street, seems to have had the mill as its main object. The great road to Charlestown may indeed have been determined in part by other considerations, such as directness and the absence of difficult hills, yet we find the roads from Woburn Centre and Richardson's Row, as well as other ancient roads, actual ways of access to Converse's mill.

The building of "Longe Bridge," August 26, 1641 (the second bridge named in the Woburn Records), it is certainly reasonable to suppose, was required by the necessity of travel to and from a mill, — not Cooke's mill, for a road to that mill was not projected till 1846, — and, if it was Converse's mill, it raises an interesting question as to the actual, location of that bridge. The saddle and pillion were used to convey the people to church and on all other occasions requiring conveyance, except "going to the mill."

In the Woburn Records, under date of "26 of 6 mo." 1641, we read: "A bridge was made across Horn Pond River: though the place was so boggy that it swallowed up much wood before it could be made passable, yet it was finished and called Longe Bridge."

Horn Pond River is the stream flowing from the outlet of Horn Pond to its junction with the Abajona, near the land of Mr. D. N. Skillings, at which point the junction is seen when the water is drawn from the millpond.

Hence at any point on the stream a bridge could be said to be "across Horn Pond River."

The bridge across this river, in the rear of Mr. Sullivan Cutter's residence, called "Blind Bridge," and so designated as early at least as the date of Edward Converse's will (see page 235 of *The Record*), was unquestionably on the road from Woburn Centre to the old mill, and must have been built at a time when Edward Converse himself was in a position of superior influence in town affairs.

But little reflection is needed to convince us that among the very earliest needs of the town would be a "bridge

across Horn Pond River" at such a point as would connect the mill and the oldest settlement in the town with the central village.

The discussion, however, of this question of the location of the " Longe Bridg" involves too much investigation, and would occupy more space than can be reasonably devoted to it in this article: therefore the writer hopes that another opportunity will be had for a fuller presentation of his reasons for hesitating to receive the common belief that it was located at the outlet of the pond at Pond Street.

As we have said, Edward Converse died in 1663. He was succeeded at the mill by his sons.

Of these sons we shall now record nothing except an account of the death of Samuel, who was killed by the water-wheel, February 20, 1669. The record of this accident is full and complete, and found in the Middlesex Court Records, file 20, 1670, paper 3.

It seems strange that this record has not been discovered before. It has never been alluded to by any historian of Woburn, and has been lost sight of by the Converse family for many years; even the date of his death is not given by Sewall in the Converse Genealogy.

It. may be claimed as a crumb of original local history brought to light by the formation of this Society.

It is satisfactory to know that at this early date, more than one hundred years prior to the Revolution, our fathers knew how to hold such inquests " decently and in order."

The papers referred to are labeled " Samuel Converse Jury." " Verdict on his death."

The first paper is the deposition of two witnesses to the accident, and reads as follows : —

" We Isaac Brooks and James Thompson being about the 21 of Feb. 69 in the Corne mill belonging to the Converses, at Wooburne, on of suddain we heard a voice about the mill wheel saying stop the wheel. upon wh. the said Thompson

did run to the mill gate & looking towards the mill wheel he
saw as he thought a man laid down and cried out my unkle
is killed. Isaak in the mean time did run to the waterwheel
and found Samuel Converse wth his head fastened between
the water wheel and water wall.

"The said Thompson in the mean time did shut the gate
and came running to the sd Brooks. Now the water wheel
being turned backwards did raise upwards and wee seeing
his head cleared went unto him and did take him up alive
who bled excessively. We did carry him into his house and
soon after we brought him in his bleeding stopt & in about
half an houres time as we conceive he was quite departed.",

"*The Verdict of the jury of quest on the death of Samuel
Converse.*

"We subscribed being by the Constable of Wooburn
Summoned a jury of quest upon the suddain and untimely
death of Seargt Samuel Convars late of Wooburne, upon
examination of the Witnesses that did take him up, going
to the place from whence he was taken up & viewing of the
Corps, doe conceive that the said Convars was cutting some
ice from off the water wheele of the corne mill & so over-
reaching with his axe was caught by his coate with some
parte of the wheele whereby his coate was rent to the
Choller thereoff & that not giving way his head was drawne
downe untill it was sucked in between the water wall & the
water wheele. now as is said he did call to shutt down the
wheele but in all probabillitie he received his mortall wound
soone after he spake to stop the Wheele. We saw much
blood in the place whereabouts he was judged to stand, also
there was blood upon the snow from the place to his house,
as is said he was carried to his house alive and being set
in a chair his blood quickly settled within him wholly preventing him from speaking & in about half an hour was
dead. We found the back side of his head greatly bruised

his nose grizzle as wee think was broken so that the said Convars his head lying as before expressed we judge his death to be by the water wheele of the Corne Mill. 22: 12: 69.

"RICHARD GARDNER	JOHN CARTER
MATTHEW JOHNSON	JOHN NORRIS
JOHN WRIGHT	INCREASE WINN
JOHN RUSSELL	JOHN MOUSALL
EDWARD IVONS	JOHN BROOKS
WILLIAM JOHNSON	WILL SYMES"

The history of the successive ownerships of the Old Mill remains to be told.

MARCH 3, 1885.   ARTHUR E. WHITNEY.

WINCHESTER IN 1640.

MY paper, read January 6, 1885, related to the character of the wilderness as described in Edward Johnson's *Wonder-Working Providence*, and the manner of commencing the new settlements, and the action of the General Court in granting additional land to Charlestown for the settlement of Woburn, with quotations from the Woburn Records from May 14, 1640, to September 30 of the same year.

" On the 5th of 9 mo," we read from the same Records, " the persons above specified were now chosen by the church of Charlestown for the carrying-on of the affairs of the new town."

We must remember that the actors were all still living in Charlestown. The persons referred to in the record just read were Edward Converse, Edward Johnson, John Mousall, Mr. Thomas Graves, Samuel Richison, and Thomas Richison. And the meetings which are recorded are held at one or another of their Charlestown houses.

On the ninth of the same month (or November 9), "these persons, associating to them Edward Johnson, who continued with them during the whole work, went to discover the land about Shawshin River; being lost were forced to lie under the rocks, whilst the rain and snow did bedew their rocky beds."

On the seventeenth of the same month (November) "a meeting was held to set a division between Charlestown and Woburne, which was in part assented to, but afterwards denied." And on the twenty-third of the same month we read : —

"The church of Charlestown meet to consider of those, that should go up to this town ; and seeing many appear, fearing the depopulation of Charlestown, from that day forward had a suspicious eye over them."

But upon the third of December, the church seems to have relented, for the entry reads thus : —

"3 of 10 mo.— Full power was given to Edward Converse and company to go on with the work."

And on the twenty-second of December we read : "Considering the weightiness of the work and the weakness of the persons, this day was set apart for humble seeking of God by prayer and fasting for help in a work of so great consequence, which was performed at the house of John Mousall, by the forenamed persons and their wives, the Lord assisting."

Four days previous to this, however, or on the eighteenth of December, we find the meeting was held at which the organization of the new town was effected.

At this meeting "Edward Johnson was appointed Recorder, who drew a plot of the town." And at this meeting "*town orders* were concluded on."

The preamble was imitated, almost copied, word for word, from that of the author of the "Liberties of the Massachusetts Colonie," attributed to Mr. Nathaniel Ward, who

might, or might not, have originally framed the noble thoughts it contains.

Mr. Ward *was*, however, the author of the code of laws which was adopted by the General Court and known as the " Liberties of the Mass. Colony." [1]

TOWN ORDERS.

" The free fruition of such liberties and privileges as humanity, civility, and Christianity calls for are due to every man, with his place and proportion, without impeachment and infringing, which hath ever been, or ever will be, the tranquillity and stability of Christian Commonwealths ; and the denial or the deprival thereof the disturbance, if not the ruin, of both."

" We hold it, therefore, our duty and safety for the better disposing of all the lands and benefits of the town of Woburne, and for the preventing of all troublesome complaints, and the maintainance of love and agreement, it is required that all persons admitted to be inhabitants in the said town shall by voluntary agreement subscribe to these orders following; upon which conditions they are admitted : —

" *First order*. For the carrying-on common charges, all such persons as shall be thought meet to have land and admittance for inhabitants shall pay for every acre of land formerly laid out by Charlestown, but now in the limits of Woburn, sixpence ; and for all hereafter laid out, twelve-pence.

" *Second order*. Every person taking lot or land in the said town shall, within fifteen months after the laying-out of the same, build for dwelling thereon, and improve the said land by planting either in part or in whole ; or surrender the same up to the town again. Also, they shall not make sale of it to any person but such as the town shall approve of.

[1] See Introduction to *Wonder-Working Providence*, p. 101. By Wm. F. Poole.

" *Third order.* That all manner of persons shall fence their cattle of all sorts, either by fence or keeper; only it is required, all garden plots and orchards shall be well inclosed, either by pale or otherwise.

" *Fourth order.* That no manner of persons shall entertain inmate, either married or other for a longer time than three days, without the consent of four of the selectmen; every person offending in this particular shall pay to the use of the town, for every day they offend therein, sixpence.[1]

" *Fifth order.* That no person shall fell or cut any young oak, like to be good timber, under eight inches square, upon forfeiture of five shillings for every such offence."

Thirty-two persons subscribed to these orders.

Edward Johnson.	Danill Bacon.
Edward Converse.	Edward Winne.
John Mousall.	Henry Belden.
Ezekill Richison.	Francis Kendall.
Samuewell Richison.	John Teed.
Thomas Richison.	Henry Frothingham.
William Lernedt.	Will Greene.
James Thompson.	Benjamin Butterfield.
John Wright.	Henry Jefts.
Michall Bacon.	James Parker.
John Seers.	John Russell.
Mr. Thomas Graves.	James Britton.
Nicholas Davis.	Thomas Fuller.
Nicholas Treerice.	Richard Lowden.
John Carter.	John Wyman.
James Converse.	Francis Wyman.

Upon the fourth of January the record reads : —

" Meeting at Edward Converse house, where were admitted many persons to set down their dwellings in this town; yet being shallow in brains, fell off afterwards. At this meeting Mr. George Bunker surrendered up his lot to the town's disposal, and had recompense."

[1] It appears by subsequent records that George Polly was severely dealt with for violating this order.

From the manner in which Mr. Bunker is spoken of we are to infer that he was not included in the class of the shallow-brained. He appears in history as the owner of Bunker's Hill, in Charlestown, and is honored by the monument which, as long as it is called "Bunker Hill Monument," will show that he was wiser than he knew in backing out of the Woburn speculation.

On the tenth of February "the first bridge was laid over the Abersonce River (later called the Abajona), "over against Edward Converse's house," and "called Could Bridg."

From the last two entries just read, we gather the following facts : —

1. That Edward Converse had, prior to the eleventh month, 1640, built and occupied a house upon this territory, which we know from various sources was near Mr. Whitney's mill, in Winchester.

2. That the meetings spoken of as held at his house were the first meetings held within the territory of Woburn, and this house the first headquarters of the town.

3. That the bridge across the Abajona at this point was the first built in the new town.

The year 1640, by the mode of reckoning then used, ended with the last day of February.

This month of February was a very busy one, as well as a cold one, if we may infer as much from the name they gave to this first bridge, " the Could Bridg."

On the eighth "the men appointed for this town affairs travelled to discover a fitting place to lay this town out. After two days search, it was by the greater number thought meet to be laid out on the east side of the land granted to this town, which accordingly was done after two days more."

On the twelfth they held a "meeting at Samuel Richison's" to consult about a minister, and admit more persons to the new town.

On the thirteenth they met at Ezekill Richison's, such as proposed to settle here, and appointed the Tuesday following (sixteenth), for meeting at the ground which had been . selected for the town, but "they received no small discouragement" from Mr. Increase Nowell, the magistrate, and the Rev. Zechariah Symmes, the minister.

On the sixteenth they came, forty of them however, to the selected place, "where," says Mr. Johnson, "the new town should have been placed, marking trees and laying bridges," but "the way being so plain backward that divers never went forward again."

On the twenty-ninth (it was leap year), " Mr. Nowell, Capt. Sedgewick, Lieut. Sprague, and some others by Charlestown appointed, advised to remove the houselots and place for the meeting-house to the place where they now stand."

Thus ends the record of 1640.

Early in the spring which succeeded, the lots of land were marked, allotted, and at once improvements upon them commenced.

. March 3, 1885.   ABIJAH THOMPSON.

OUR ABORIGINES.

Some notice of the natives found in occupancy by our forefathers properly belongs to our history.

By some law or freak of association, which it might be difficult to define, we are reminded, while reading up "authorities" upon these aborigines, of the "house that Jack built." One builds upon another, others upon their predecessors, until a mass of literature accumulates which promises abundant light, while it gives but little, as to the ethnological or ethnographical questions involved. We have insufficient data for determining whether these Indians,

most commonly called Pawtuckets, are in any degree akin
to the Mound-builders, from whom they may have degener-
ated, or to the Iroquois, or to other of the conjectural race-
divisions. Neither skull, color, feature, traditional customs,
nor languages afford any satisfactory answers to questions
such as are plausibly successful respecting most other grand
divisions of mankind.

We must be content with the fragments of observation
left by those who first looked upon them on these shores
and in these forests.

The terms "Aberginians," "Abergenymen," "Abarginny-
men," and the like, in the earliest mention of the natives
of Massachusetts, seem, by some bungling corruption of the
word "aborigines," to have denoted only the savages at
large.

John Smith (1614) designates those found on this coast
as the "Massachusetts," and estimates their number at about
three thousand (Mass. Hist. Coll. xxxvi, p. 119); describing
them as a "well-proportioned people." Wood, in his tract
entitled "New England's Prospect" (1634), describes the
"Aberginians"; and Bancroft (vol. iii, p. 3) quotes his
description as follows: —

"First of their stature, most of them being between five
and six foot high, straight bodied, strongly composed, smooth
skinned, merry countenanced, of complection more swarthy
than Spaniards, black haired, high foreheaded, black eyed,
out-nosed, broad shouldered, brawny armed, long and slender
handed, out-breasted, small waisted, lank bellied, well
thighed, flat kneed, handsome grown legs, and small feet.
In a word, take them when the blood brisks in their veins,
when the flesh is on their backs and marrow in their bones,
when they frolick in their deportments and Indian postures,
and they are more amiable to behold (though only in Adam's
livery) than many a compounded Phantastick in the newest
fashion."

It will be remembered by the readers of *The Record* that Captain Edward Johnson, arriving in 1630, with Winthrop's company, betook himself at once to the Indians for purposes of trade, and was exceptionally well acquainted with them during his life. It is refreshing to be able to turn from the dull iteration of authorities, to be found in the town histories all around us, to the very graphic though quaint observations of Captain Johnson, in which the citizens of Woburn and Winchester may properly feel a family interest.

On page 15 of the *Wonder-Working Providence* he writes of a well-known incident in the following picturesque style: " Not long before, the whole Nation of the *Mattachusets* were so affrighted with a Ship that arrived in their Bay, having never seene any before, thus they report: some persons among them discerning a great thing to move toward them upon the Waters, wondering what Creature it should be, they run with their light cannowes (which are a kind of Boates made of Birch Rindes and sowed together with the rootes of white Cedar-Trees), from place to place, stirring up all their Countreymen to come forth and behold this monstrous thing: At this sudden news the shores for many miles were filled with this naked Nation, gazing at this wonder, till some of the stoutest among them manned out these Cannowes, being armed with Bow and Arrowes, they approached within shot of the Ship, being becalmed, they let fly their long shafts at her, which being headed with bone, some stuck fast, and others dropped into the water, they wondering it did not cry, but kept quietly on toward them, till all of a sudden the Master caused a piece of Ordnance to be fired, which stroke such feare into the poore *Indians*, that they hasted to shore, having their wonders exceedingly increased ; but being gotten among their great multitude, they waited to see the sequell with much amazement, till the Seamen firling up their salies came to an Anchor, manned out their long bote, and went on shore,

at whose approach the *Indians* fled, although they now saw they were men, who made signes to stay their flight, that they may have Trade with them, and to that end they brought certaine Copper-Kettles; The *Indians* by degrees made their approach nearer and nearer till they came to them, when beholding their Vessells, which they had set forth before them, the *Indians* knocking them were much delighted with the sound, and much more astonished to see they would not breake, being so thin: for attaining those Vessells they brought them much Bever, fraughting them richly away according to their desires."

With respect to the tribes which dwelt upon our particular territory, it is noticeable that, while others describe them as the *Pawtuckets*, he does not anywhere, in his frequent mention of them, employ this designation, although he has much to say of the "Mattachusetts," the "Nianticks," the "Pequods," the "Narrowgansits," the "Tarratines," and others. The only passage in the *Wonder-Working Providence* which has the form of ethnological description is the following, on page 16, where he is speaking of the desolating sickness which occurred about 1613–16 : —

" The *Abarginny*-men, consisting of *Mattachusets, Wippa-naps*, and *Tarratines*, were greatly weakened, and more especially the three Kingdoms, or *Saggamore* ships, of the *Mattachusets*, who were before this mortality most populous, having under them seven Dukedomes, or petty *Saggamores*, and the *Nianticks* and *Narrowgansits*." " The *Pecods* were also smitten at this time."

Gookin, Massachusetts Historical Collection, i, p. 149, — an authority accepted by Frothingham and others, — represents the Pawtuckets as a distinct nation from the Massachusetts, separated by the Charles River, the latter extending south and west, and the former occupying the territory as far as the Piscataqua River on the east and northward to Concord on the Merrimack.

The subdivisions of the Pawtucket tribe Mr. Gookin gives as "Pennakooks, Agawomes, Naamkeeks, Pascatawayes, Accomintas, and others," each of which divisions (or dukedoms, as Johnson has it) was under a distinct saggamore; the great sachem, or king, being Nanepashemit.[1]

The form of government of these tribes was patriarchal and hereditary, as we may infer from the history of Nanepashemit's family as it has been preserved by our forefathers. This king at his death left a widow, Squa Sachem, and three sons, the widow becoming queen of all the Pawtuckets, and the sons saggamores; as, Wonohaquaham, or Saggamore John of Mystic; Montowampate, Saggamore James of Lynn; and Wenepoyken, Saggamore George of Salem, the latter of whom became, after the death of Squa Sachem, the grand sachem of the Pawtuckets, about 1684.[2]

The most succinct and pithy description of the character of this Indian government is given by the spiteful Thomas Morton, of Merry Mount notoriety, in his book entitled *The New English Canaan*, printed at Amsterdam, 1637, in which he says of the Indians: "They may be accounted to live richly, wanting nothing that is needful, and be commended for leading a contented life, the younger being ruled by the elder, and the elder ruled by the Powahs, and the Powahs are ruled by the Devill, and then you may imagine what good rule is like to be amongst them."

As to their domestic life and martial traits it is not our present purpose to speak further than to quote one or two passages from our own redoubtable Johnson.

In describing the reception of the "Solemne Embassage" at "Cannonicus Court," 1637, of which Johnson was a member, he says: "They were entertained royally with respect

[1] See article on Squa Sachem, *Record*, l, p. 19.
[2] Lewis's History of Salem.

to the Indian manner. Boiled Chestnuts is their White-bread, which are very sweet, as if they were mixt with Sugar; and because they would be extraordinary in their feasting, they strive for variety after the English fashion, boyling Puddings made of beaten corne, putting therein great store of black befryes, somewhat like Currants. They having thus nobly feasted them, afterward gave them Audience· in ·a State-house, round, about fifty foot wide, made of long poles stuck in the ground, like your Summer-houses in England, and covered round about, and on the top with mats, save a small place in the middle of the Roofe, to give light, and let out the smoke.

"The Indian Sachim lay along on the ground, on a Mat, and his Nobility sate on the ground, with their legs doubled up, their knees touching their Chin: with much sober gravity, they attend the Interpreter's speech." [1]

The following passages form significant pictures of their martial traits : —

"They [the colonists] send forth a band of Souldiers, who, arriving in the *Peaquod* Country, address themselves to have a Treaty with them about delivering up the murtherers; they making shew of willingness so to doe, bade them abide a while and they would bring them, and in the mean time they were conversant among the Souldiers, and viewing their Armie [armor] pointed to divers places where they could hit them with their Arrowes for all their Corslets." Having obtained this information, the Indians "shewed the English a fair pair of heeles, . . . saying, Englishman's God was all one Flye, and that English man was all one Squawe, and themselves all one Moor-hawks." [2]

"The English . . . concluded to storm the fort a little before break of day; at which time they supposed the

[1] Wonder-Working Providence, p. 109.
[2] *Ibid.* p. 111.

Indians being up late in their jolly feasting, would bee in their deepest sleep." They approached the fort, "which was builded of whole Trees set in the ground fast, and standing up on end about twelve foot high, very large, having pitcht their Wigwams within it; the entrance being on two sides, with intricate Meanders to enter." The English "found the winding way in without a guide where they soon placed themselves round the Wigwams and according to direction they made their first shot with the muzzle of their Muskets downe to ground, knowing the Indian manner is to lie on the ground to sleep." Then follows an account of the slaughter in the fort and a battle with the main body at a little distance from it; "the Squawes crying out, 'Oh, much winn it Englishmen!' who moved with pitty toward them Saved their lives; and here up on some young youth cryed: 'I squaw, I squaw!' thinking to find like mercy. There were some of these Indians, as is reported, whose bodyes were not to be pierced by their sharp rapiers or swords of a long time, which made some of the Souldiers think the Devil was in them, for there were some *Powwowes* among them which work strange things with the help of Satan." "One of them [the English] being shot through the body, neere about the breast, regarding it not till of a long time after, which caused the bloud to dry and thicken on eitheir end of the arrow so that it could not be drawne forth his body without great difficulty and much paine, yet did he scape his life and the wound healed."

While French philosophers and poets, in the distance, eagerly proclaimed the discovered solution of all great social problems in the simplicity and beauty, the purity and innocence, of these unsophisticated children of nature, those who knew most of them were saying, in the devout (?) language of Johnson, "They knew right well that till this cursed crew were utterly rooted out, they should never be at peace."

" Poor Lo ! " has his poetic aspects and attitudes, and his claims upon those who have appropriated his forests and prairies, lakes, rivers, and hunting-grounds, indefeasible in the atmosphere of Christian charity and civilization. Yet his is no saintly race, and the term " savage " (Old English " salvage," meaning, " belonging to the woods " — from *silva,* " wood ") came by no unnatural process to represent men, as well as wild beasts, characterized by cruelty, ferocity, brutality.

The few traditions and relics of the race supplanted here in " Waterfield " pertain mostly to deeds of savage cruelty or the implements of war.

The following incident is recorded in Richardson's Memorial, by Vinton (p. 119) : —

" Mr. Samuel Richardson, son of Samuel, one of the first settlers, lived on Richardson's Row " (his house still standing within the recollection of our older citizens, a few rods north of the present residence of Mr. Samuel G. Bodge).

" In the afternoon of April 10, 1676, he was employed in carting manure in his field accompanied by his son Samuel, a boy between five and six years old. Looking toward his house, he was surprised at seeing feathers flying about it and other tokens of mischief within. He also heard the screams of his wife. Apprehending that Indians might be there, he hastened home with his gun, and there found two of his family murdered, namely, his wife Hannah, who had been lately confined, and his son Thomas, twin-brother to him who had been with him in the field. On further search, it was found that the infant, only a week old, had been slain by the same ruthless hands. The nurse, it appeared, had snatched it up in her arms upon the alarm of danger, and was making her escape to a garrison-house in the vicinity; but so closely was she pursued by the savages, that, finding she could not save herself and the babe too, she let the babe drop, and the Indians dispatched it at once. Mr. Richard-

son now rallied some of his neighbors, who went with him in pursuit of the enemy. Following them some time, they espied three Indians sitting on a rock, fired at them, killed one, and drove the others away."

The history of King Philip's War abounds in incidents of equal barbarity. The sentiments governing their hostile movements seem, as a rule, to be less reasonable, and more cruel, than can be illustrated in the ravages of the most ferocious wild beasts. The fighting impulse, love of inflicting torture, and indolent habits of the males, scorning the labor imposed upon the females, are the traits out of which our estimates of the Indian character are chiefly to be formed. The exceptional lights in the dark picture are analogous to such as one sometimes notes in beasts of prey.

Many of the families of Winchester are descendants of those who lived in continual peril, who, as Trumbull expresses it, "asleep or awake, at home or abroad, were in constant jeopardy."

Among the mementos of the tribes that dwelt upon our Winchester soil are the arrow and spear heads, stone hatchets, and pestles, occasionally found, and doubtless many families have gathered such relics while tilling the ground in the vicinity of Mystic and Horn Ponds, which were evidently favorite haunts of the Indians.

Some have found their way to the cabinets of our Society. A short time since a nest of arrow and spear heads was found on Pine Street, near the residence of Mr. Henry C. Whiten, by the workmen engaged in laying water-pipes. Their being thus found in a cluster would indicate a probability that they were buried with the brave to whom they belonged, in accordance with a general custom among the Indians, as well as with the well-known Indian conception of his need of arms and food for his long journey beyond the grave. It does not appear that a grave was in this instance actually opened, although, as the superin-

tendent of the water-works informs the writer, there were indications of a portion of a grave thus cut into.

A singularly beautiful but small stone hatchet has been presented to the Society by Mr. Joel F. Hanson, which was found upon the Wentworth farm. This may, from its diminutive size and especially careful working, so as to preserve a symmetrical arrangement of the stripes in the rock, have been designed for an ornament rather than a practical cutting instrument.

A heavy stone pestle for pounding corn has been presented by Mr. William E. Boynton, which was found upon his land between Wildwood Street and Church Street, which was shaped to be held by a withe in a wooden handle, like an axe.

Traditions represent that the Indians continued to visit this region even after they were driven to distant parts. Frothingham, in his History of Charlestown, assigns one of the residences of Squa Sachem to Gardner's Row (Cambridge Street), and the stream of water which takes its rise near the schoolhouse in the Hill District, flowing down the valley west of the Bartlett place, through the lands of the late Stephen Swan and Edmund Dwight, and into Mystic Pond, has borne the name of Squa Sachem's Brook.

Stephen Swan (deceased in 1871, aged eighty-six) frequently said to his children that his father (John Swan, born 1734) spoke of the yearly visits of the Indians to this brook, where they would remain a few days. They had planted certain roots and herbs upon the banks of this stream, evidently for medicinal purposes. They often came to his house in a friendly manner. Also he relates that the Indians had the custom of passing up from the tide-water through the Mystic Ponds on to Horn Pond, where they encamped and remained during some part of the warm season.

This custom was in fact continued to a comparatively

recent date, — even after the completion of the Middlesex Canal.

Mrs. Cyrus Butters remembers, and many others may also remember, the Indians coming up through the Middlesex Canal, remaining at the "Lock House" over night; moving their canoes, tents, and other baggage around the locks upon their backs.

These locks were near a point on Everett Avenue, and also near the old home of Mrs. Butters (the old Edward Gardner house, on Gardner's Row, now occupied by Mr. John Swan), and in plain sight from the house. The "Lock House" was that built for the tender. The encampment of these Indians was, one year in her recollection, on the land where our High Schoolhouse now stands.

Hannah Shiner, or Squa Shiner, was an Indian woman whom our old families had occasion to know about, and who seemed to have become a solitary waif from all tribal relations, to subsist upon the curiosity and crumbs of Winchester civilization; her case being (race and kindred excepted) not entirely without a parallel in our more modern history. She lived alone, part of the time, in a hut by a spring upon the eastern margin of Turkey Swamp, where she made baskets and "Indian trinkets" for sale, when not employed among the families in mending chair-bottoms, or other services, in *quasi*-compensation for the broken food she could obtain. At another time she is remembered to have lived in an old house, long since disappeared, at the corner of Church and Bacon Streets, and is described by some who remember her, as she appeared to their childhood, as short and small in stature, with a thin face, traveling about with a little dog, which, when she called at a house, she was accustomed to hide under her skirts, in a manner very amusing to the children. She, too, had the habit of visiting the Squa Sachem Brook, and the Swan family, who dwelt by it. On one cold winter day, while crossing the old

Converse bridge, in a high wind, her slight form was blown from it into the water and she was drowned.

Thus the legend, as told by a lady whose family was best informed of the appearance and the disappearance of this relic of the aboriginal occupants of Winchester. Though not so romantic as the disappearance of the "Last of the Mohicans," yet, doubtless, many a young lady among us may be able to frame from these few elements a picturesque and pathetic tale of the "Last of the Pawtuckets." Undoubtedly the range of verisimilitude and poetic conception is about as wide as such work ordinarily requires. That our soil contains the dust of numbers once living upon it, whose deeds of bravery and scenes of love-making threw a glamour over these beautiful lakes and their surrounding scenery, is .beyond a doubt, though no necropolis has yet been opened.

The only Indian grave assuredly testified (so far as the writer is informed) is that of a child, — a bill for whose coffin is cited in favor of S. & F. H. Johnson, and for the interment of the same in favor of Josephus Johnson, in our Town Report for the year 1852. Doubtless a child of a strolling band, who sickened and died here, and whose remains were cared for as a public charity.

As attention may be awakened, much more may be added to our meagre local Indian history.

Edward Converse, in his will, speaks of "Indian Hill" (in Winchester). The ground thus designated is to be identified and the reason to be explained.

SEPTEMBER 5, 1885.   GEORGE COOKE.

THE HEADS OF FAMILIES IN WINCHESTER IN 1680. — TITHING–MEN.

EVERYBODY has heard of the tithing-men, who in the early times of our towns were appointed to have the oversight of their neighbors, and to see that they kept good order in their houses. To enable them to perform their office, all the inhabitants were distributed into companies of ten adjacent families each, inclusive of the family of the overseer, or tithing-man; a number or company of ten families, giving the meaning to the word. These tithing-men appear in Woburn in 1676, and were all men of the first respectability in the town.

A note on page 49 of Sewall's History of Woburn has suggested the idea of a way of getting information of the names of the heads of the families of the district now Winchester in 1680. The note is as follows: "At a meeting of the Selectmen, 5 of 5 mo [5 July], 1680, nine persons are named as Tithing-men, and the names of all the heads of the families (82 in all) which were severally assigned to them for their inspection in their respective districts. — Town Records, vol. ii, pp. 153, 154."

By referring to the original records, we find the following, which we copy; the ten families in the first group all belonging to the part of Woburn now in Winchester.

"5 of 5 mo, 1680.[1] persons appointed for the inspection of decon Josiah Conuers as tithing-man : —

" John Howlton.	Nathanell Richardson.
Sam^ll Richardson.	Capt Carter.
Steeuen Richardson.	Eusigne Conuers.
Widow Richardson.	John Carter."
Izack Richardson.	

The following group is partly in Winchester, or on its border : —

[1] Town Records, vol. ii, pp. 154, 155.

"persons appointed for the inspection of Sargent Mathew Johnson as tithing-man: —

" Izack Brooks.	John Brooks.
John Berbeane.	William Johnson.
John Greene.	Sarg^t Jams Conuers.
Sargent Thomas Peirce.	Jacob Hamlett."
Henry Brooks.	

W. R. CUTTER.

HISTORY OF THE ROADS OF WINCHESTER PREVIOUS TO 1850.

GROVE STREET.

THE first plan of Grove Street on record was made in 1705. It is to be found in the Probate Office at East Cambridge, and a copy of this plan belongs to the Winchester Historical and Genealogical Society.

The road was probably used at the first settlement of the country. It was the only road to the farm granted to Zechariah Symmes previous to 1640. He had a farm and mill, and this must have been the road to get to it.

At the first settlement of the country, they used the rivers as highways. Medford was at the head of navigation on the Mystic. Iron, salt, and West India goods were landed at the Square. The hay, seaweed, rockweed, and kelp, for manures of their farms, were brought in boats as near to the farms as possible, then taken in carts to the land. The first landing was at Rock Hill, near High Street, formerly Grove Street, and near the house of the late Mr. Edmund Hastings. It was here that Nanepashemit landed, in 1615, when he retreated from Saugus after the great war with the Tarratines.

" In 1619, four years after, they besieged his fortifications at Rock Hill on the Mystic, where, after a most heroic resistance, Nanepashemit was killed."

The next landing, or ford, was in Winchester, at Bacon's Bridge. The people who lived on the farm where Mr. John H. Bacon now lives had to cross the Abajona River by a ford to go to Boston and Cambridge. John Symmes and family went to meeting at West Cambridge, and went by the way of Grove Street.

Tradition says that they did not put on their stockings and shoes until they had crossed the stream, — then they put them on.

When Edward Convers, Edward Johnson, and others, in 1640, went up the country to locate the town of Woburn, they must have taken this road.

In an old deed, dated 1795, the piece of land described was bounded on the northwest by the road leading to Cambridge. By another old deed a piece of land was bounded by the road leading from the post-road to Weir's Bridge, both referring to Grove Street.

CAMBRIDGE STREET.

In 1643 Edward Convers and Ezekiel Richardson, of Woburn, and Captain Cooke, of Cambridge, were chosen a committee to lay out a street from Woburn to Cambridge.

We find that in 1641, August 26, the people of Woburn built a bridge over Horn Pond River. The place was very boggy and swallowed up much wood. They called it Long Bridge. (Sewall.) The road that the committee laid out must have been the road now called Cambridge Street, as far as Pond Street, thence by Pond Street across the above-mentioned bridge to Woburn.

Although in 1646 the town of Woburn laid out a street from Woburn by the house of Joseph Gardner to Cooke's mill, and called it Plain Street, Joseph Gardner lived on the west side of Woburn, on the road to Lexington. It will be seen that it was much farther than by Horn Pond.

CHURCH STREET.

The town of Woburn in 1646 voted to lay out a road from the King's Ford, over and against the house of Edward Convers, to Plain Street. It was to be two rods wide, one rod to be taken from Mr. Symmes and one rod from Mr. Convers. The King's Ford was where the bridge now stands, near Mr. Whitney's mill. Plain Street is now called Cambridge Street. This road was called Driver's Lane, and was used for driving cattle to the pastures on the west side of the town.

WASHINGTON STREET.

In 1647 a committee was appointed to lay out a road from the three Richardsons to the meeting-house in one direction, and to Mr. Thomas Graves's house in another. The three Richardsons lived on Richardson Row, as it was called, — now Washington Street. This road to the meeting-house, I think, is Cross Street. The town record does not tell where Mr. Graves lived. The Rev. Samuel Sewall, in his History of Woburn, says he did not own a house, and thinks he lived here temporarily, as his name was not in the list of freemen.

HUTCHINSON'S ROAD, OR FRUIT STREET.

In 1802 the town of Charlestown chose a committee to report on the encroachments on the roads. Among others was Hutchinson's Road. The report of the survey says the road was laid out two rods wide, from Mr. John Hutchinson's to Mr. Seth Wyman's, but Mr. Hutchinson's *cow-yard* encroached one rod; at the other end Mr. Daniel Reed had encroached seven feet.

RIDGE STREET.

This was an old road, but 1 can find no record of its being laid out previous to 1850. The same with High Street.

FOREST STREET.

This was a narrow crooked lane, and I think there was no laying out previous to 1850.

MAIN STREET.

In 1646 provision was made to construct a road from Woburn to Mystic Bridge, Medford. The present Main Street, from Woburn to Winchester, follows the old road as far as the house of Mr. Stephen Cutter; from there the old road went around the meadows by Mr. Joseph Hunnewell's across the stream, back of the house of Mr. Sullivan Cutter; then crossing Main Street at right angles, it ran back of the houses of Messrs. P. W. Swan and Edmund Sanderson; thence Main Street to Symmes Corner. Grove Street was used to go to Medford, as the town of Medford did not lay out the lower part until 1747. In that year Medford voted to lay out a road from the Great Bridge (same as Mystic Bridge — or Craddock Bridge, as it is now called) to Woburn. It was called the Great Road. The celebrated Black Horse Tavern was situated on this Great Road, on Black Horse Hill. Previous to 1810 the county commissioners caused the Great Road to be straightened, from Mr. Stephen Cutter's mill to the house of Mr. Edmund Sanderson, by filling the meadows and bridging the two streams. The bridge, now built of stone, was called Blind Bridge;[1] the other has since been taken away and the stream filled.

BACON STREET.

About 1828 the county commissioners laid out a road from Symmes Corner to Church Street. A causeway was filled across the pond, and willow-trees planted on either side. It was a very pleasant street until the Boston and Lowell Railroad, to avoid a grade crossing, built a bridge over their road, and made the steep hill which now has to be climbed to get over it.

[1] Were there two bridges designated as *Blind Bridge?* If so, which one was intended in Edward Converse's will? — ED.

THE SOUTH WOBURN SOCIAL LYCEUM.

DURING the autumn of the year 1846 an interest began to be manifested among some of the young people of South Woburn on the subject of mutual and social improvement. After talking the matter over informally for some little time, and suggesting various ways by which the desired objects could be best attained, several of those most interested in the subject met at the house of Deacon B. F. Thompson, for the purpose of further discussing the proposed question.

This meeting was held on the evening of the nineteenth of October, 1846, at which time and place the society was formed and a constitution and by-laws adopted. The rules were few and simple, and officers were chosen rather more for formality than for any honors that might accrue or any arduous duties that might be imposed. No one was to retain an office more than three months, so that all, officers and others, might take part in the exercises and share equally in its duties and honors, such as they were. In fact, it was a strictly democratic institution on a small scale.

The society was called "The Social Lyceum," and had for its objects literary and social improvement. Its exercises consisted in reading selections from prose and poetry, original compositions, discussions, conversation, and the cultivation of the social faculties generally. At some of the earlier meetings vocal music was sometimes introduced. Young men could join the society by receiving a vote of two thirds of the members and paying into the treasury a small sum, merely to defray incidental expenses. Ladies could become members by receiving a two-thirds vote and subscribing their names to the constitution.

At the first meeting, the following officers were elected: Andrew N. Shepard, President; Walter M. Brackett, Vice-president; Abijah Thompson, Secretary and Treasurer.

The society met once in two weeks, and the meetings were generally held at private dwellings, for the purpose of encouraging a greater degree of sociability, and also to keep the expenses within moderate limits. The details and written reports of the society are not now accessible, neither are the compositions, of which quite a number were presented and read by the writers or by the presiding officer. They all reflected due credit on the authors, especially those written by the ladies. To these essays the society listened with great interest.

Notwithstanding the records of the society are so meagre, and its written documents cannot be produced, this much, at least, can be said: a good many valuable selections were read, quite a number of interesting compositions were written, and a few subjects discussed. Among the latter were the following: "Was the invention of gunpowder a blessing to mankind?" "Is woman in her proper sphere when actively and publicly engaged in the reforms of the day?"

For various reasons the society did not continue in existence for a very long period, certainly not over a year. After the novelty of the affair had somewhat worn off, and some of the members had removed from town, and others were removed by death, the interest in the objects of the society began to diminish, and the attendance became quite small. Finally a singing-school was opened in the village, which attracted the attention of most of the members, when the meetings were discontinued, and the society came to an end.

But notwithstanding its brief existence, there is no doubt that much good was the result of its organization in various ways; chiefly, perhaps, in forming a better acquaintance with each other, and in cultivating literary tastes and capacities, which, in later years and under different circumstances, produced more conspicuous results; though it may be doubted whether any more enjoyable or satisfactory.

The following are the names of the members: —

Andrew N. Shepard.
Walter M. Brackett.
Abijah Thompson.
Samuel B. White, Jr.
William Henry White.
Benj. H. Shepard.
Theodore P. Rogers.
Kanellum W. Baker.
Cyrus Blood.
William P. Walker.
George R. Starkey.
Edward A. Fesssenden.
Josiah Gilman.
R. F. Knights.
—— Mansfield.
—— Parker.

Lydia L. Hutchinson.
Eliza A. Hutchinson.
Lavinia J. Rogers.
Rebecca A. Rogers.
Susan F. Whittemore.
Maria S. Swan.
Eliza A. Swan.
Lucy A. Doane.
Esther B. Newcomb.
Luthera Teele.
Martha Wilder.

SAMUEL B. WHITE, Jr.

WINCHESTER, June 17, 1885.

Mr. Teel, having applied for membership, writes the following: —

"JAMAICA PLAIN, ROXBURY, August 26, 1846.

"To the Members of the Society for Mutual Improvement of Young Men, — Next Friday night being the time to which you adjourned at the last meeting in March, I shall not be able to attend, but I will write a line to you to let you know my feelings on the subject. I hope, for one, that we shall be able to succeed in this work that we have begun. I mean to be there the first Friday in October, and I will try to do what I can to keep it up. Keep it a-moving; we have got hold, and let us keep hold and never let go. The only way we can get along is to persevere. Never mind that singing-school; whoever wants to attend that can do so besides. We have a long winter before us and a good chance for improvement for all that I can see, and as for any changing of the constitution, I will go as the majority says. About a library, as was talked of by some, — I think we have

not got along far enough for that, but as the majority goes I will go.

"Rouse up, ye boys of South Woburn, and put a sound in every corner of the old schoolhouse that shall take the shine off the old National Theatre itself!

"Yours respectfully,

"WARREN TEEL."

Nearly forty years afterward Mr. Teel, having been written to for recollections of those early days in South Woburn, wrote the following letter: —

"DAVENPORT, IOWA, March 30, 1885.

"*Dear Mr. Thompson,* — Your letter of the twenty-fifth instant came to hand last Saturday, and contents noted. I wish I could recall what you desire to know about the old events that transpired in the *long, long* ago, when Winchester was South Woburn, and was familiarly called Black Horse Village. But as I grow old and the farther end of the 'long path' comes in sight, the events that transpired in dear old Woburn came vividly before me, and Winchester seems all a blank.

"Away back in the thirties I can see your dear old father and mother, then comparatively young people, living in what was to me a palace, on Pleasant Street, near the General's. I can see them both, and you and Martha, and the old pew in Father Bennet's church. I also remember the very day you all removed to South Woburn, having been preceded by S. S. Richardson, who removed from the foot of Academy Hill.

"Perhaps I may be so fortunate as to have something about these new events in old South Woburn come to me. I shall have what you want to know upon my mind the next few weeks, and if anything offers to me, will note it down and send to you. All seems a blank to me now. John Gilson,

machinist; Joe Sharon, woodworker; a Mr. Adams, Usher's son-in-law; Alvin Taylor; E. A. Brackett, sculptor, and Dr. Piper and Warren Teel were among the members of Dr. Youngman's Society. *Where, when*, and *who* met with us, I cannot recall. Still, it may yet come to me; if it does, I will let you know.

" If my dear old sister Lucy were alive, how much she could tell you about the early settlers of South Woburn, and Sol. Fletcher. A history of South Woburn without Solomon in it were like the play of Hamlet with Hamlet left out.

" When I have tried to think of something the last twenty-four hours about what you want to know, my mind comes right *whack* on to S. S. Richardson.

" I have a good anecdote to tell about him, which you might insert in your history. It is a funny one. Well, I will give it to you soon.   Truly yours,

"WARREN TEEL."

Since receiving the above letter, Mr. Teel has sent us the following

REMINISCENCE.

On the last Wednesday of May, in the year 1835, fifty years ago, the first car conveying passengers, drawn by a locomotive on the Boston and Lowell Railroad, passed through Black Horse Village on its way to Lowell.

Notice had previously been given that the great event was to take place on old " election day," which, in the old time, occurred always on the last Wednesday in May. It was an occurrence of great importance, and the people, young and old, along the route from Boston to Lowell, gathered to the line of the railroad to see this new wonder. I was then a lad of seven years, and, with the others, gathered at the clump of birches just below the old mill on the Thomas Richardson place — the old mill where your

Mr. Harrison Parker and brother Asa used to cut up mahogany. All " Richardson Row " was there ; the houses along the road to Reading, in this part of the town, were deserted; with patience they waited for the wonder to appear. That you may know how little was their knowledge about railroading, I will relate an incident that occurred while waiting for the train.

For a small boy I had quite an engineering turn of mind, and for days I had pondered over this scheme of running wagons on a rail by steam. What seemed uppermost in my mind . was how thick a substance could be successfully placed upon the rail without incurring an accident to the train. I laid awake nearly all the night before, revolving in my mind what I might put on the rail the next day to test the experiment. I privately concluded that an old Bungtown copper cent would be *the thing.* But, alas, how few mortals are equal to the situation ! When the news arrived that the cars were coming in sight my courage failed, but not until Col. Samuel White, who was present on the occasion, had detected me in trying to place the coin on the rail; where-upon he roundly rated me upon my hazardous venture ; still, being a little curious himself, he compromised the matter by loaning me an old-fashioned fourpence half-penny (6 1-4 cents). It being well worn and very thin, he thought there would not be much risk, so I boldly marched up to the track, and, before all the crowd, placed it upon the iron rail, and breathlessly waited for the huge monster to come along. Various were the emotions in my breast those few moments. I am happy to state that remorse overtook the Colonel and myself about the same moment, and we both vied with each other in our haste to remove the obstacle from the track. After having accomplished this we felt: that is, I did: we were good enough to go straight to heaven if we died that moment. But I should not be doing the Colonel justice if I did n't now state that, to the best of my recollection, he was

the first to remark after the engine and car passed: "Sho! you might have put a silver dollar on the rail and no harm come of it!"

This was half a century ago. Now, here on these Western prairies, we run over a Texas steer and don't know it until the bill comes for damages to the steer. .

WARREN TEEL.

DAVENPORT, IOWA, April 10, 1885.

PARISH RECORDS.[1]

AT a meeting of the inhabitants of the South Village in Woburn, held at the Wakefield House, May 12, 1840, for the purpose of taking into consideration the importance of . forming a new religious society, Mr. Zachariah Symmes, 2d, was chosen chairman, and Benjamin F. Thompson, secretary.

The subject having been thoroughly discussed, it was voted that it is expedient to form a new religious society, to be called the Woburn South Congregational Society, provided a sufficient number of persons can be obtained to afford a good prospect of success.

Benjamin F. Thompson, Loring Emerson, and Sumner Richardson were chosen to procure names in addition to those present, and report at an adjourned meeting.

May 19, 1840, at the adjourned meeting the committee reported a list of names of those persons who wished to become members of said society. All present were called upon personally to answer the following question: Shall we proceed to a regular organization of said society? All present answered in the affirmative.

Benjamin F. Thompson, Stephen Cutter, Stephen Swan, Alvah Hatch, and Sumner Richardson were chosen a com-

[1] Transcribed from vol. i, p. 1.

mittee to take the necessary steps for a regular organization of said society.

The meeting was then dissolved.

B. F. THOMPSON, *Secretary.*

PETITIONING FOR A WARRANT.

To Col. Leonard Thompson, Justice of the Peace, in and for the County of Middlesex, — You are hereby requested to issue a warrant for a meeting of the legal voters of the South Congregational Society in Woburn, for the purpose of organizing said society by the choice of officers, and other necessary business, namely : — .

To see what measures the Parish will take to erect a House of Worship, or do anything in relation to the same.

To see what measures the Parish will take to procure necessary Funds to defray the expenses of building a Meeting-house and other expenses of said Parish.

To see if the Parish will procure a lot of land to locate the Meeting-house on, or do anything in relation to the same.

To see if the Parish will procure Musical Instruments, or do anything in relation to the same.

BENJAMIN F. THOMPSON,   ALVAH HATCH,
STEPHEN SWAN,   SUMNER RICHARDSON,
STEPHEN CUTTER,

Petitioners.

WARRANT ON THE FOREGOING APPLICATION.

To Benjamin F. Thompson, one of the Members of the South Congregational Parish in Woburn, in the County of Middlesex, — In the name of the Commonwealth of Massachusetts, you are required to notify and warn all the members of said Parish qualified by law to vote in said Parish, to meet at the schoolhouse, in Ward No. 6, at three o'clock P.M., on Monday, the first day of June next, to act upon the following articles, namely : —

ARTICLE 1. To elect all such officers as may be wanting to serve the Parish the ensuing year.

ART. 2. To see what measures the Parish will take to erect a House of Worship, or do anything in relation to the same.

ART. 3. To see what measures the Parish will take to procure the necessary funds to defray the expenses of building a Meeting-house and other expenses of said Parish.

ART. 4. To see if the Parish will procure a lot of land to locate the Meeting-house on, or do anything in relation to the same.

ART. 5. To see if the Parish will procure Musical Instruments, or do anything in relation to the singing in said society.

And you are hereby directed to serve this warrant by notifying personally every member qualified to vote in said Parish, or by leaving at his place of abode a notification expressing the time, place, and purposes of said meeting, seven days at least before the time appointed for the same. Hereof fail not, and make return of this warrant with your doings thereon to the said meeting at the above time and place.

Given under my hand and seal, and dated at said Woburn this twenty-second day of May, A.D. 1840.

LEONARD THOMPSON, *Justice of the Peace.*

WOBURN, June 1, 1840.

·Pursuant to the within warrant, I have notified and warned all the members of said Parish, qualified by law to vote in said Parish, to meet at the time and place, and for the purposes specified in said warrant.

BENJAMIN F. THOMPSON.

Proceedings at a meeting for the organization of the Woburn South Congregational Parish and the transaction of

other business June 1, 1840, holden in the schoolhouse Ward No. 6.

The Petition, warrant, and answer to the warrant were read by Col. Leonard Thompson, Justice of the Peace.

1. The vote for clerk was called for by Col. Leonard Thompson; and Sumner Richardson was chosen, and qualified by taking the necessary oath before the chairman.

2. Zachariah Symmes, 2d, Moderator.

3. Voted to choose a Parish Committee of three. Chose Stephen Cutter, John Fiske, Harrison Parker, Committee.

4. Voted to choose assessors on one ballot. Chose Loring Emerson, Joseph Wyman, Luther Elliott, Assessors.

5. Chose Benjamin F. Thompson, Treasurer.

6. Chose Samuel B. White, Collector.

7. Voted to choose two Auditors. Chose Nathan B. Johnson, Stephen Symmes, Auditors.

8. Voted to build a Meeting-house.

9. Voted to choose a committee of seven to build the house. Chose Benjamin F. Thompson, Stephen Swan, Harrison Parker, Henry Cutter, Marshall Wyman, Nathan B. Johnson, Sumner Richardson, Committee.

10. Voted that those persons who have subscribed for pews be requested to pay to the Treasurer twenty-five dollars on or before the first day of July, and those who are willing be requested to pay more.

11. Voted to authorize the Treasurer to hire one thousand dollars and give his note in behalf of the parish.

12. Voted that the Committee build such a house as they think proper, not exceeding five thousand dollars, including land and every expense.

13. Voted that the Building Committee be authorized to procure a lot of land for building the house upon.

14. Voted that the singing be referred to the Parish Committee.

15. Voted to take up Article 3 again.

16. Voted to raise such sums of money as the parish may need for parish purposes by subscription.

17. Voted that the assessors be a committee to procure the above subscriptions.

Attest,   SUMNER RICHARDSON, *Parish Clerk.*

Transcript of names of members in the order in which they stand (vol. i, pp. 4 and 5, and vol. ii, pp. 350–353).

NOTE.—The * indicates deceased members. This designation is not copied from the records, but supplied from information obtained while the article is in press.—ED.

*Benjamin Franklin Thompson.
*Nathan Brooks Johnson.
*Joseph Wyman.
*Samuel Symmes.
*Isaac Shattuck.
*Marshall Wyman.
*Eli Kendall.
Stephen Cutter.
*Francis Johnson.
*Henry Cutter.
*Francis Johnson, Jr.
*Stephen Nichols, 2d.
*Rei Hills.
*Alvah Hatch.
*Jesse Richardson.
*S. Stanley Wyman.
*John H. Coates.
*Job A. Davis.
*Josiah Stratton, Jr.
George Sanderson.
*Samuel Steele Richardson.
Oliver Richardson Clark.
*Stephen Symmes.
*Joseph B. Symmes.
*Matthew Griswold.
*Horatio Symmes.
*Jeremiah Watson.
*Stephen Swan.
*John Fisk.

Andrew Cutter.
*Nathan Jaquith.
Harrison Parker.
John G. Richardson.
*Isaiah Reed, Jr.
*Luther Elliott.
*Samuel B. White.
*John Hathaway Richardson.
*George Eaton.
Sullivan Cutter.
*Zachariah Symmes, 2d.
Sumner Richardson.
*Johnson Symmes.
*Calvin Richardson, Jr.
Gardner Symmes.
*William Pierce.
John Buxton.
Stephen H. Richardson.
*Caleb Richardson.
*Loring Emerson.
*Jefferson Ford.
*Caleb Richardson, Jr.
*Thomas Richardson.
*John G. Usher.
*Charles W. Stevens.
*James Bell.
*John Cutter.
William Richardson.
Samuel Smith.

*Putnam Emerson.
*Thomas Hutchinson.
*A. W. Goodell.
*James H. Shepard.
Stephen Symmes, Jr.
Moses C. Greene.
*Samuel Kendall.
*Thomas Collins.
*Charles Russell.
Stephen H. Cutter.
Horace Hatch.
Salem T. Ward.
Joseph Symmes.
Lucius B. Nutting.
*John Whittemore.
*John Ayer.
*Samuel M. Rice.
*Francis H. Johnson.
*Joseph Hunnewell.
*Charles Pressey.
Joseph Huse.
*James Bridge.
John N. Randall.
*Alvin Taylor.
John C. Worthen.
John A. Cram.
Charles Hall.
*W. W. B. Lindley.
*Peleg Lawrence.
Isaac Holmes Kendall.
*Richard W. Piper.
*Zebadiah Abbott.
*Nathan Blanchard.
*William A. Dodge.
*Joseph B. Blanchard.
*William A. Warren.
A. N. Shepard.
Charles W. Wilder.
Luther Richardson.
*James T. Langley.
David Youngman.
*Samuel Kendall.
Abijah Thompson.

Elizabeth Richardson.
*Phebe Bell.
*Nancy B. Eaton.
Lucy Sellers.
*Clarimond Wyman Pierce.
Delia Pierce.
*Hannah Wyman.
*Mary Cutter.
*Josiah Walker.

Since 1850.

Samuel S. Holton.
Jonathan Clark.
*Abel Houghton.
Joseph Stone.
Edwin A. Fessenden.
*Asa Fletcher.
*Alonzo Chapin.
Stephen A. Holt.
James R. Bayley.
J. C. Johnson.
*Reuben T. Robinson.
Elmore Johnson.
*Josephus Johnson.
E. W. Clark.
William D. Maxwell.
John T. Manny.
*Joshua Lane.
Lemuel Holton.
Warren Coffin.
Alfred Norton.
Samuel B. White, Jr.
Thomas P. Tenney.
*S. T. Sanborn.
*Abel Green.
*Phillip Kelley.
Robert Crawford.
*Charles Goddard.
Henry Stone.
Edmund Sanderson.
*Alvan Cheney.
*J. C. Roberts.
*A. E. Bates.

*David Nelson Skillings.
*Thomas V. Holton.
Stephen Thompson.
Allan F. Boone.
George H. Chapman, Jr.
Justin Lawrence.
Sylvester G. Pierce.
A. W. Quimby.
Daniel W. Kimball.
Edward H. Rice.
*James H. Prince.
S. B. Pratt.
Charles O. Shephard.
W. C. Redfern.
George Rice.
Thomas Shepard.
Levi C. Ela.
Charles F. Lunt.
Charles E. Conant.
*H. K. Thatcher.
Robert Cowdrey.
Charles W. Underhill.
Oliver R. Clark, Jr.
Joseph H. Tyler.
M. A. Herrick.
H. F. Clark.
*Edwin Lamson.
James F. Dwinell.
P. W. Swan.
Leone S. Quimby.
Warren Johnson.
Andrew Allison.
Edward F. Sanborn.
Marcus C. Cook.
I. S. Palmer.
F. W. Prince.
Henry A. Emerson.
Benjamin Bray.
Henry F. Johnson.
George G. Stratton.
Wm. P. Greeley.

Cyrus W. Blood.
A. E. Rowe.
Harrison Parker, 2d.
J. W. Hemingway.
George Cooke.
John S. Richardson.
A. K. P. Joy.
Edwin Robinson.
George McDaniel.
John Winslow Richardson.
Warren F. Foster.
Zenoni A. Richardson.
J. F. Stratton.
James P. Boutwell.
J. W. Skillings.
Eugene Tappan.
Arthur Fletcher.
Joseph W. Guernsey.
Frank M. White.
Edward H. Stone.
Charles E. Redfern.
Alfred S. Hall.
Walter V. Smalley.
E. S. Osgood.
Benjamin T. Church.
C. H. S. Foster.
Emmons Hatch, Jr.
Preston Pond.
Alfred C. Vinton.
George E. Rogers.
Samuel J. Elder.
Charles Nelson Dodge.
John Reed Cobb.
George H. Carter.
Charles E. Swett.
Samuel Usher.
William H. Herrick.
Handel Pond.
Thomas F. West.
George D. Rand.
William Ladd Dodge.

EDWARD H. RICE, *Parish Clerk.*

WINCHESTER, June 27, 1885.

THE CONGREGATIONAL CHURCH CHOIR.[1]

SOUTH WOBURN, 1840–1853.

THE Congregational Society at South Woburn was organized May 19, 1840. Its house of worship was built during the same year, and dedicated the last day but one of the year, December 30, 1840. During this interval religious services were held generally at the red schoolhouse, nearly opposite the present Baptist Church, and the preachers were, for the most part, theological students from Andover. The Rev. Luther Wright, of Woburn, called "Father Wright," officiated occasionally, and obtained some of the preachers.

There was no regularly organized choir in the place at that time, nor, as a matter of fact, until several years later. But wherever religious services are held singers can generally be found. Such was the case at that time. Quite a number of persons of musical tastes and talent volunteered their services, and, meeting frequently for practice and rehearsal, and also assisting at the services of the sanctuary, a society, containing a respectable number of good singers and musicians, soon came into existence, formed, as such societies often are, from the exigencies of the case.

On the Town Records of Woburn, under date of 1840, appears a petition signed by B. F. Thompson, Stephen Swan, Stephen Cutter, Alvah Hatch, and Sumner Richardson, embracing the following, among other articles desired to be inserted in a warrant for a public meeting, namely: " To see if the Parish would purchase musical instruments, or do anything in relation to the same, for the South Congregational Parish."

[1] This paper probably contains inaccuracies, as the writer had no memoranda of any kind, but was obliged to trust to memory in relating events that took place many years ago. He takes this opportunity to express his thanks to Mr. Stephen H. Cutter for furnishing important facts and incidents occurring previous to 1846. D. Y.

Mr. Stephen Cutter, a prominent and well-known citizen of South Woburn, had for many years led the singing at social and religious meetings held at the South Parish; and he now became the leader of this recently formed choir, after the organization of the new society, — selecting the tunes, and directing the music with his violin. He performed the same duties for many years afterward, whenever the regular chorister was absent. With such a record, Mr. Stephen Cutter, who still survives at the venerable age of eighty-eight years, must be regarded as the first leader and conductor of the South Woburn Church Choir.

Mr. Joseph Gould, a citizen of the place, — a manufacturer at Bacon's Bridge, and a man of fine musical taste, — had been leader of the choir at Woburn for a year or two. He taught a singing-school in 1838–39, in the hall of the famous Black Horse Tavern; and also taught another the following winter, that of 1839–40, at the red schoolhouse, which was attended by most of the singers residing in the village, some of whom had been members of his choir at Woburn.

Mr. Gould was a good teacher and an excellent singer, and under his direction and training the new choir made special preparation for the exercises at the approaching dedication; and when that day arrived, assisted by some members of the celebrated Peak family from Medford, and other musical artists who kindly volunteered their assistance, performed the service of song on that occasion to the general satisfaction of the large audience.

Mr. Gould was now employed by the parish, for a stipulated amount, to lead the choir and conduct the music in the new church. He had an excellent voice, and generally sung the tenor; but, if occasion required, could sing the soprano equally well. He also played skilfully on the violin, with which he usually accompanied his voice. Possessing such qualifications, he made an efficient and popular leader, and remained in that capacity for two years — 1841 and 1842.

During Mr. Gould's first year of service another important
event occurred that should not be omitted.   The ordination
of the first settled pastor, the Rev. George P. Smith, took
place June 17, 1841, on which occasion the choir, under the
direction of Mr. Gould, performed the musical portion of the
services, and fully sustained the reputation it had earned
at the dedication, six months previously.

The choir, during these two years, consisted of about
twenty members.   Prominent among them was Miss Almira
Johnson, daughter of Deacon Nathan B. Johnson, afterward
the wife of Mr. Stephen H. Cutter.   She was the leader of
the soprano, and by her strong, full voice, together with a
requisite degree of confidence, sustained her part and gave
strength and efficiency to the whole choir.   She possessed,
also, what is essential in a leading singer, promptness and
punctuality, being always present and always reliable.   She
retained this prominent and responsible position in the choir
for many years.

Miss Clara Fisk, daughter of Mr. John Fisk, afterward
wife of Mr. Waterman Kimball (now Mrs. Chandler, and a
widow, residing in Boston), was leader of the alto.   She had
a strong, heavy voice, and yet it was pleasant and well
adapted to the singing of duets and solos.   She sung for
about three years, — during Mr. Gould's terms of service and
a part of his successor's, Mr. Trowbridge, — fully sustaining
her part during that time.   She left the choir in 1843,
greatly regretted.

Mr. John Fisk, a resident at the "West Side," had been a
member of the choir at Woburn for many years.   He had a
heavy voice, of round, full tone, and, when the new society
was formed, became the recognized leader of the bass, and
continued to give efficient aid and encouragement for five or
six years, retiring in 1846.

Other members of the choir (of whom it is impossible to
speak further than mention their names) were as follows:

Philip Bryant, Job A. Davis, Francis Johnson, Jr., Alvah Hatch, Eli Kendall, Andrew N. Shepard, Charles W. Stevens, Salem T. Ward, William A. Warren, and Walter Wyman.

The ladies' names were as follows: Mrs. Linda (Richardson) Buxton; Mrs. Mary Ann (Kendall) Ward; Mrs. Nathan Jaquith, Jr.; Miss Adaline A. Cutter, afterward Mrs. Charles Hall; Miss Nancy Eaton, afterward Mrs. J. B. Judkins; Miss Abigail Richardson, afterward Mrs. Josiah Stratton, Jr., and Miss Eliza Ann Swan, afterward Mrs. James T. Langley, now Mrs. Samuel R. Smith.

It does not appear that there were many musical instruments in the choir at that time besides the leader's violin and that of Mr. Stephen Cutter. Mr. Waterman Kimball played the violino, or double bass viol, and sometimes the violin. Mr. Eli Kendall occasionally played the violoncello or single bass.

Mr. Gould was succeeded by Mr. Asa R. Trowbridge, of Newton, who was employed as leader in 1843. He was a composer and teacher of music, played the violin, and had a good tenor voice. He taught a singing-school in the vestry of the new church the following winter. He remained leader of the choir only one year, but during that time a large number became connected with it. Besides the names of the original members already given, the following appear during this year: —

Stephen H. Cutter, William A. Dodge, Sylvanus Elliot, John S. Fisher, Charles Hall, Edward F. Kendall. Isaac Holmes Kendall, Hatevil K. Stanton, Alvin Taylor, and the Hon. B. Frank Whittemore.

The ladies' names were: Mrs. Samuel W. Twombly; Miss Eliza J. Kendall, afterward Mrs. John A. Cram; Miss Maria S. Swan, afterward Mrs. Abijah Thompson; Miss Lucy A. Doane, afterward Mrs. Frederick Beck; Miss Harriet N. Johnson, and the Misses Hutchinson.

The instrumental music at this time was somewhat varia-

ble. Mr. Stephen Cutter continued to play the violin. Mr. John Buxton had succeeded Mr. Kimball on the violino. Other instruments fell into line as opportunity or inclination dictated. William A. Warren sometimes played the tenor trombone; Stephen H. Cutter, Andrew N. Shepard, and Isaac Holmes Kendall played the flute. Mr. John S. Fisher played the violin, and sometimes the orchestral serpent. The ophicleide, bassoon, clarinet, and bugle were heard occasionally in the choir.

During the year 1843, the choir was formally and regularly organized ; but as the book of records is not now accessible, it is impossible to give the details, or even the names of the officers.

Mr. Pendergrass succeeded Mr. Trowbridge as musical director and leader of the choir in 1844. He had a full, pleasant tenor voice, and was accustomed to sing songs and solos with much effect. His singing of " The Grave of Bona-parte " is still remembered with great pleasure. Nothing of special note occurred during this year ; and the choir remained practically the same as it had been for two or three years, although some of the original members began to drop off. Mr. Pendergrass remained only one year, and was succeeded by Mr. Alvin Taylor in 1845.

When the writer of this paper settled in South Woburn, March, 1846, the choir was composed of a dozen or more members, of average musical talent; and it compared very favorably with the choirs of neighboring parishes. It was led by Mr. Alvin Taylor, who was also leader of the bass. He was a very good singer, accurate and reliable, with a good voice and good address, and he made an acceptable leader for an ordinary country choir.

He was senior partner with Mr. Edmund Sanderson, and kept what was called a " country store," in the building now owned and occupied by Mr. B. F. Holbrook. Their store was afterward kept in " Richardson's Building," where Mr.

Taylor remained till his death, and where Mr. Sanderson still remains. Mr. Taylor was also postmaster, the second one, I believe, appointed at South Woburn, — Dr. Moses C. Greene being the first. He was also treasurer of the town of Winchester for three years. Mr. Taylor was a very worthy man, rather conservative, of correct habits, and a very useful member of society. He died in the prime of life, of consumption, November 21, 1859.

After Mr. Taylor's term of service as chorister expired, in 1846, the present writer was engaged as leader and conductor of the choir, and was paid a small salary by the parish. He taught a singing-school in the vestry of the church the following winter, that of 1846–47, which was largely attended ; and also another in the same place and with similar success in the winter of 1847–48. He continued to lead the choir for about six years, until a short time before the large organ was placed in the church, in 1852.

During those years several important events occurred that called for special musical exercises on the part of the choir. Prominent among them was the installation of the second settled pastor, the Rev. William T. Eustis, Jr., which took place April 8, 1846 ; and the ordination of the third settled pastor, the Rev. John M. Steele, August 10, 1848. On these occasions the choir sustained its former reputation by making appropriate selections and performing music adapted to, and designed for, such occasions. The services at the ordination of the Rev. Mr. Steele were particularly interesting from the preaching of the sermon by the venerable president of Dartmouth College, the Rev. Nathan Lord, D.D.

The following persons were members of the choir, for longer or shorter periods, during the half-dozen years from 1846 to 1852, brief notices of each one of whom will be given according to the best recollections of the writer.

Mr. William A. Warren was a prominent member of the choir in 1846. He sung on the bass, and had a good, reliable

voice. He was a currier by trade, and a very worthy man.
He left town in 1870, removing to Lunenburg, where he
still resides.

Mr. Andrew N. Shepard was another reliable bass singer.
He was also a currier by trade, and lived in town till
1881, when he removed, and now resides in Nashua, New
Hampshire.

Mr. Salem T. Ward, who still resides in town, was also a
conspicuous member of the choir, singing also on the bass.

There were also the brothers Kendall, Edward F. and
Isaac Holmes, who, if not so celebrated as their namesakes,
the famous " Ned " and " Jim " of the old Boston Brass
Band, yet filled important places in our choir. Edward F.
had a full, heavy bass voice, and added much to the strength
of that part. He left town in 1858, and lived about two
years in Portland, Maine, when he removed to Mobile,
Alabama, in 1860. He came North during the war, and
afterward returned to Alabama, where he now resides.

Isaac Holmes Kendall sung also on the bass, and sometimes played the flute. He still resides in town, and is
employed at the pianoforte manufactory of Cowdrey, Cobb,
Nichols & Company. He has been for many years, and
still is, the efficient and popular sexton of the Congregational
Church.

Their father, Eli Kendall, sung in the choir occasionally.
He had previously, for a short time, played the violoncello.
He was a practical musician, and had been a manufacturer
of melodeons and other musical instruments. He died in
1860.

Mr. Asa Fletcher joined the choir in 1845 or 1846, and
sung till 1864. He was a good tenor singer, and quite
regular in his attendance. He died November 17, 1880.

Mr. Michael McClary Steele, a brother of the pastor, sung
in the choir for a year or two. He had a good tenor voice,
and, had he made vocal music a specialty under the direc-

tion of modern instructors, would doubtless have become a distinguished singer. He now resides at Epsom, New Hampshire, on the old McClary estate.

Mr. Josiah Hovey joined the choir in 1849, and sung about two years, when, at the organization of the Baptist Church, he left and identified himself with the choir of that society. He became its leader, and remained in that capacity about eleven years. He was a good bass singer, and made an efficient and popular leader.

In 1856 he purchased the apothecary-store of the present writer, and continued the business about nine years, when he sold out to Mr. George P. Brown, and engaged in manufacturing a preparation for the hair, in which he was quite successful. After Mr. Brown built his new store, in 1880, Mr. Hovey reopened the original one in Lyceum Building, where he still remains engaged in his legitimate business.

Mr. Hovey was elected town clerk for nine consecutive years, from 1856 to 1864 inclusive. He was also appointed postmaster in 1866, and held the office about five years.

Nor must I omit to mention another important and rather conspicuous member who sung with us for several years. Mr. Ebenezer Smith, having purchased a summer residence on Church Street, came to South Woburn in 1847 or 1848. Though past middle age, Mr. Smith was one of the most enthusiastic of men. He was an old-fashioned tenor singer, and his cheerful presence was always inspiring and encouraging. He was particularly interested in stenography, and would sit with his tablets and take down the entire sermon in shorthand.

Mr. Smith was a patron of art and music; was a member of the Handel and Haydn Society. Upon the advent of Jenny Lind, he was a large purchaser of tickets for the mere encouragement of song. Mr. Smith was wealthy and quite liberal, though in a quiet, unostentatious manner. I am told that he was one of a number who contributed

$1,000 each for the relief of Daniel Webster. He was, withal, somewhat peculiar and eccentric. He once said to me: "I never let my left hand know what my right hand does." After the rebuilding of the church in 1854, a fine tower clock was presented to the society from some unknown friend. It afterward transpired that it was given by Mr. Ebenezer Smith. The extent of his private charities may never be known. He was always silently giving and quietly relieving the aged and the poor. He died in Boston, in 1864.

Of the ladies, Mrs. Almira (Johnson) Cutter, who had been one of the most prominent and faithful members of the choir from the beginning, still retained that responsible position, and was the acknowledged leader of the soprano. She fully sustained her part, and remained, giving efficient aid and strength to the choir, during most of the time the present writer had charge of it. In the summer of 1849 she left, temporarily, on account of illness, and did not return till the autumn of 1852, at the introduction of the new church organ. She then resumed her former prominent place in the choir, and remained about fifteen years longer, making a combined term of service of nearly twenty-five years, — a term longer than that of any other member of the choir, excepting her father-in-law, Mr. Stephen Cutter. During all those years she gave her valuable services to the choir, and aided and encouraged it on all occasions by her commanding voice and presence, until she finally retired in 1868, much to the regret of the singers and the entire congregation. She died October 5, 1881.

Miss Lucy A. Doane was leader of the alto at that time. She joined the choir in 1843, at quite an early age, and remained about four years, leaving it at the close of 1846. She had a remarkably fine mezzo-soprano voice, and became distinguished as a vocalist in later years. After removing to Boston, she was first a pupil of the famous Dr. Lowell

Mason, and sung in his choirs for some time. She afterward became a pupil of that "sterling artist and sweet tenor singer," August Kreissmann, and assisted in the performance of Handel's "Alexander's Feast," in the spring of 1849, the first time the piece was performed in America, under the direction of the celebrated George James Webb. She sung several years at the Rev. Mr. Coolidge's church, on Harrison Avenue, and about five years at Dr. E. E. Hale's, on Union Park Street. In 1859 she married Mr. Frederick Beck, now treasurer of a copper company, No. 68 Devonshire Street, Boston, and resides in Brookline.

Miss Harriet Newell Johnson, a younger sister of Mrs. Stephen H. Cutter, had joined the choir in 1843 or 1844, and continued to give valuable aid by singing the alto. She became leader of that part after the departure of Miss Doane. She had a very fine alto voice, and though not particularly strong or full, it was sweet and pleasant, and, had she lived, would doubtless have become a superior singer. But failing health compelled her to leave the choir in 1856, and she died of consumption, September 23, 1858.

Miss Abigail Richardson, one of the original members of the choir, still remained, a valuable and reliable soprano singer. In 1848 she married Mr. Josiah Stratton, Jr., and is now a widow, and resides at the old homestead.

There were also the sisters Hutchinson, one of whom, Lydia L., married Cyrus W. Blood, and another, Elizabeth C., married Varnum P. Locke, and both still reside in town. The Hutchinsons were a family of singers; and if not so celebrated as their famous namesakes of New Hampshire, they deserve to be noticed in the reminiscences of the town. The family was frequently invaded by death, one after another being cut off prematurely by that fatal scourge of New England — consumption.

Miss Ellen M. Burnham, afterward Mrs. Aaron D. Weld,

joined the choir in 1848, and sung about four years. She had a full-toned average alto voice, and sung that part with confidence and efficiency. After the formation of the Baptist Society she left our church and united with that in 1857. Her husband, Mr. Weld, died in the army, at New Orleans, in 1862. She remains a widow, and still resides in town.

Her sister, Miss Annie Burnham, afterward Mrs. Rev. John M. Steele, and now Mrs. Henry Johnson, of Lynn, sung the soprano in our choir for a short time.

Miss Susan Warland, now Mrs. Caleb Winchester, of Peabody, sung the alto for some time, together with Miss Ellen M. Burnham.

The Misses Swan, already mentioned, still remained members of the choir; and if not so frequently seen in their places as some others, they were none the less welcome.

Mrs. Salem T. Ward also continued to be a constant and valuable member.

The following ladies joined the choir between 1847 and 1851: Miss Lavina Rogers, now Mrs. Sylvanus Elliot; Miss Nancy W. Cutter, now Mrs. Stephen A. Holt; Miss Martha J. Alden, now Mrs. J. T. Beers; Miss Susan F. Whittemore, who removed from town and afterward married, and now lives in Newburyport; Miss Martha D. Wilder, who died in early life, of consumption, and Miss Amanda Kimball, who also died quite young.

Miss Elizabeth Steele, sister of the pastor, became a member of the choir in 1849, and sung two or three years. She had a strong, full, alto voice, and was leader of that part most of the time she remained. She also played the organ occasionally, in the absence of the regular organist. After the formation of the Baptist Society, she sung for a while in the choir of that church. In 1855 she married Mr. J. Lincoln Bangs, a flour merchant living in Cambridge and doing business on Long Wharf, Boston. About three years afterward they removed to Montreal, where they resided twenty-one years.

During a part of that time Mrs. Bangs sung in the choir of the Church of the Messiah. Her husband died about five years ago. She now resides in Cambridge.

Miss Martha J. Alden joined the choir in 1850, and remained about one year. She had a full, strong, alto voice, with a mezzo quality. She went to Boston, and in a few years became noted as a quartette singer. She became a pupil of several musical artists of distinction, and sung three years at the Rev. Mr. Fuller's church, on Hanover Street, and then two years at Park-street Church. She afterward became a pupil of the celebrated August Kreissmann, and sung five years at Dr. Hale's church. She also sung five years at the Episcopal Church at Brookline, and from one to two years each at several other churches, making an aggregate of over twenty years as a quartette choir-singer. In 1860 she married Mr. Jacob T. Beers, and still resides in Boston.

The musical instruments, though not numerous or especially conspicuous, were very well proportioned to the number and capacity of the choir. Mr. John Buxton continued to play the violino, thus giving ample support and efficiency to the bass. He still resides in town, and is employed at the furniture manufactory of S. C. Small & Co., Nos. 71 and 73 Portland Street, Boston.

Mr. Stephen Cutter continued to play the violin; and although he did not attempt to vie with Ole Bull, he yet played our simple church tunes as well, perhaps, as that celebrated artist would have done. He had ever manifested great interest in the choir, was always in his place, and continued for many years the acknowledged leader at evening and other services, in the absence of the chorister.

Mr. Stephen H. Cutter, a member of the firm of S. and H. Cutter & Co., played the flute, and blended its sweet notes harmoniously with his father's violin and Mr. Buxton's heavier violino. Like his father and his wife, he could

always be relied on, in all kinds of weather and on all occasions.

Mr. Andrew N. Shepard and Mr. Isaac Holmes Kendall each played the flute occasionally, and thus gave additional strength and variety to the orchestra.

After the reconstruction of the church, in 1850 and 1851, a small parlor pipe-organ was placed in the gallery, and Mr. James A. Woodbury, the machinist and inventor, was employed for a short time as organist. His melodious and tasteful interludes are still remembered with pleasure by many who heard them thirty-five years ago. Mrs. James A. Woodbury also, for the time being, gave us the valuable aid of her fine soprano voice, which efficiently strengthened and encouraged the whole choir.

At the time the small organ was introduced, Mrs. Deacon Zebediah Abbott became a member of the choir and the leader of the soprano. She remained till the large organ was placed in the church, in 1852. She had a strong, musical voice, and made a very excellent soprano leader.

After Mr. Woodbury left, Mr. Francis Hazeltine, from Chester, N. H., played the small organ, and led the choir for a year or so. He was a teacher of music by profession, and made a very good conductor.

In 1852 a fine organ, built by Messrs. Simmons & McIntier, was placed in the church; and Mr. James C. Johnson, who had recently removed from Boston and settled in town, was engaged as organist and musical director. He continued his services in that capacity, to the entire satisfaction of the choir and parish, for more than seventeen years.

It is hoped and expected that Mr. Johnson will soon contribute a paper, giving his reminiscences of the choir during the time he had charge of it, thus furnishing a complete and continuous history from its commencement to the present.

DAVID YOUNGMAN.

THE ANXIOUS SEAT.

[From the *Woburn Guide Post.*]

GAYLY the choir began to sing
  In the church of Fountain Street,
    As a stranger beau
    Essayed to know
  If he could find a seat.
In vain he cast his eyes around;
  No sexton crossed his path,
No empty pew therein he found,
  And he thought of turning back.
In vain he sought, that anxious beau,
Through all the galleries and below;
He stood a sad, unseated thing,
And now the choir had ceased to sing.

Young blooming converts filled the air
  With sighs and glances sweet;
    And he edged his way,
    As they rose to pray,
  Up to the anxious seat.
A sister fair, in robe of white,
  The stranger came to greet —
She asked him if he 'd "found a hope,"
  And offered him a seat.
" Oh, lady fair! " the stranger cried,
"No hope is mine, save at thy side;
Give me a place, then, I entreat,
Beside thee on the anxious seat."

A kerchief to his eyes he pressed.
  In deep concern of mind
    She asked to know
    If the stranger beau
  Was " seriously inclined."
No word he said — she raised her head —
  And lo! she wept alone —
Her 'broidered kerchief, edged with lace,
  And the anxious beau were gone!

Now, when she lures with glances sweet
Pale strangers to the anxious seat,
She eyes them with a cautious gaze,
And always watches while she prays.

APRIL 29, 1847.

ADVERTISEMENTS.

DECEMBER 10, 1846.

LEVEE AND SALE. — The Female Emancipation Society of South Woburn intend holding a levee and sale on Tuesday, December 15, in the vestry of Rev. Mr. Eustis's church, for the purpose of obtaining money to be appropriated to the Canada Mission. We are informed that the Marion Band have kindly volunteered their services, and that in addition there will be songs and glees to contribute to the occasion. Tickets can be obtained at A. Taylor & Co.'s store, South Woburn, and at the door; price of single tickets, twelve and one-half cents; family tickets, twenty-five cents each. Here is an opportunity for the friend of the slave to contribute to his comfort, and at the same time to derive other pleasure besides that which a sense of having done good will furnish.

OCTOBER 15, 1846.

CHESTNUT POSTS. — Five hundred prime chestnut posts, for sale by A. N. Shepard, South Woburn.

FEBRUARY 11, 1847.

Notice is hereby given that I have sold to my son, Samuel H. Davis, Jr., his time from and after this day, and that I shall henceforth claim none of his earnings nor pay any debts of his contracting.

SAMUEL H. DAVIS.

WOBURN, February 1, 1847.

MESSENGER'S NOTICE.

MARCH 4, 1847.

MIDDLESEX, ss. — Notice is hereby given that a warrant has been duly issued by S. P. P. Fay, Esq., Judge of Probate, a Master in Chancery within and for the County of Middlesex, against the estate of Ira L. Gove, of Woburn, cabinet-maker, an insolvent debtor; and the payment of any debts or the delivery of any property by him are forbidden by law. A meeting of the creditors of the said insolvent will be holden at the Probate Office, in the City of Cambridge, in said county, on the eighth day of March next, at ten o'clock A.M., for the proof of debts and the choice of one or more assignees to said estate.

ALBERT THOMPSON, *Messenger.*
WOBURN, March 5, 1847.

ACCIDENTS.

OCTOBER 1, 1846.

A sad accident occurred last week at South Woburn. Mr. Josiah Symmes, who was engaged in excavating a well on his grounds, having occasion to descend into it, to adjust some stones at the bottom, was buried beneath several feet of earth, which, owing to the insufficiency of the curb, fell in upon him. Three hours elapsed before any direct efforts could be made to extricate him, and eighteen before he was got out. He left a wife and child.

DECEMBER 10, 1846.

RAILROAD ACCIDENT. — Just after the last train for Woburn had left the depot at South Woburn, but before it had got much speed on, the engine ran off the track, dragging with it the tender and one of the passenger-cars half-way, in consequence of the switch being wrong. No one was injured.

OUR VILLAGE BELL.

BY B. B. STANTON.

I HEAR its voice move softly through
    The silent night,
When talking to itself of the flight
Of time, and how it ever flew!
To careless ears its words ne'er change;
    But O how strange
Their meaning to my own; its chime,
The heart-beat of expiring time!

And when the holy Sabbath comes,
    In solemn mood,
To lead our thoughts from earth to God,
I hear its voice of silv'ry chimes
Float through the air. It seems to say:
    "Come up and pray,
That every heart may know its God;
And knowing, bend and kiss His rod!"

When death's hand seals another soul,
    Its iron tongue
Between its iron lips is swung
To soothe us with its solemn roll!
Oh, may its sympathetic toll
    Upon my soul
Ever vibrate, with a melancholy swelling —
Of the eternal city ever telling!

WINCHESTER, May 12, 1859.

2.

3.

1.

4.

5.

TOWN CLERKS.

1. Dr. David Youngman, 1850–55.
2. Josiah Hovey, 1856–64.
3. George P. Brown, 1865–72.
4. Warren F. Foster, 1873–82.
5. George W. Spurr, 1883–

TOWN HISTORY.

SOME PRELIMINARY MEASURES FOR THE ORGANIZATION
OF THE NEW TOWN.[1]

AT a meeting of citizens residing in South Woburn,
December 17, 1849, a committee of eight persons was chosen
to obtain a list of names by which to designate the contem-
plated town, and report at an adjourned meeting.

Chose: Benjamin F. Thompson, John A. Bolles, Harrison
Parker, Samuel B. White, Samuel S. Richardson, Francis
Johnson, Josiah Hovey, and Charles Pressey.

December 24, 1849. The above committee made the
following report: —

Since the appointment of your committee, circumstances
have occurred (of a character which renders it improper for
us to do more than allude to them) which induce us, instead
of reporting a list of names, to recommend that a committee
be chosen who shall be empowered to decide upon a name,
and insert it in the petition to the Legislature.' These circumstances are both personal and pecuniary, and promise to
be of material importance to the welfare and convenience of
the new town and its citizens.

All of which is respectfully submitted.

        For the Committee, BENJAMIN F. THOMPSON.

On motion, *Voted,* That this report be recommitted, with
instructions to report six names forthwith. *Voted,* That
Frederick O. Prince be added to the committee.

After a short deliberation, the committee reported the following names: Appelton, Avon, Channing, Waterville, Winchester, Winthrop.

Voted, To instruct the committee of three, who were
chosen at a previous meeting to present the petition to the

[1] From the minutes of the secretary of the several meetings held for this object.

Legislature, to select one of the above six names and insert the same in the petition.

The committee reported the name of *Winchester*, and the same was adopted.

At the meeting February 14, 1850, a committee was chosen to confer with any committee that may be chosen by the town of Woburn in regard to the division line between Woburn and the proposed new town.

Chose: Nathan B. Johnson, Sumner Richardson, and Benjamin F. Thompson.

A committee of four was chosen to invite the Legislative Committee on Towns to visit the proposed new town, and to entertain them in a suitable manner.

Chose: Charles McIntire, Nathan B. Johnson, John A. Bolles, Oliver R. Clark.

On the twenty-ninth day of January, 1850, an order of notice was served upon the Town Clerk of Woburn to call a town meeting to see what action the town would take upon the petition of E. S. Parker and others; and the following record of that meeting is copied from the Woburn Town Records by Mr. Nathan Wyman, the Town' Clerk of Woburn : —

"At a legal meeting of the Inhabitants of the Town of Woburn holden at the Town Hall on Thursday the 7th day of February, A. D. 1850, the following votes were passed, namely : —

" 1. Chose William T. Grammar, Moderator.

" 2. *Voted*, That the town is willing that the prayer of the petitioners should be granted on just and equitable terms, said terms to be agreed upon by a committee mutually chosen from each part of the town, and they to report at an adjourned meeting.

" *Voted*, That the chair appoint a committee of five to nominate a committee of six.

" The chair appointed Bowen Buckman, Stephen Nichols, Zachariah Richardson, Oliver R. Clark, and Dana Fay.

" *Voted*, To sustain the nomination of the chair. And they reported the names of the committee as follows: Cyrus Thompson, Bartholemew Richardson, Horace Conn, Benjamin F. Thompson, Nathan B. Johnson, and Sumner Richardson.

" *Voted*, To accept the report.

" *Voted*, That when we adjourn this meeting we adjourn till 2 P.M. next Thursday.

" *Voted,* To reconsider the vote whereby we voted to choose a committee of conference.

" *Voted*, To dissolve this meeting.

" A true Record.

" NATHAN WYMAN, JR., Town Clerk."

A true copy from the Town Records of the Town of Woburn, vol. xvi, p. 87.

Attest,   NATHAN WYMAN, JR.,
Town Clerk of Woburn.

The foregoing copy of the record fails to give a correct idea of the character and conduct of that meeting, hence the following particulars [2] are furnished to supply the deficiency : —

At the beginning of the meeting Mr. Oliver R. Clark offered a resolution in these words, namely: " *Voted*, That the town is willing that the prayer of the petitioners be granted." This was discussed very fully, fairly, and calmly by Messrs. Oliver R. Clark, John A. Bolles, Benjamin F. Thompson, L. P. Davis, and Jesse Mann, in the affirmative, and in the negative by Messrs. Horace Conn, Cyrus Thompson, John Tidd, Albert Thompson, Bartholomew Richardson, John Cummings, Stephen Nichols, Jr., and N. A. Richardson.

An amendment was added by Mr. Clark himself in these words: " Upon just and equitable terms, said terms to be agreed upon by a committee to be chosen from each part

---

[1] From secretary's records.

of the town, who shall report at an adjourned meeting." With this amendment the vote was passed with great harmony, and the chairman was directed to appoint, and did appoint, five gentlemen to retire and nominate a committee of six in pursuance of Mr. Clark's resolution.

While the nominating committee was out the time arrived for the departure of the last railroad train for South Woburn, and many of the South Woburn voters, who had attended the meeting in large numbers, departed for their homes.

After they had gone and before the nominating committee made their report, Mr. Horace Conn moved that a committee be raised to appear before the Legislative Committee and oppose the petition. The chairman, after some exciting debate, decided that the motion was out of order. It proved to be the signal of a course of conduct on the part of the meeting alike dishonorable and disorderly. The nominating committee reported the committee of six for the conference, and their report was accepted.

Mr. Horace Conn was of the number, but instead of declining to serve, he renewed his motion to raise a committee and employ counsel to resist the petition. It was again ruled by the chairman that this motion was out of order until the former vote was reconsidered. Mr. Conn then withdrew his motion, and a resolve was offered by Mr. Sewall that the meeting reconsider the vote by which the committee of conference was chosen.

In the midst of great uproar this vote passed, and then Mr. B. F. Thompson moved a dissolution of the meeting, which was carried. It was at once perceived by Mr. Conn and his party — but too late — that the reconsideration had not, after all, changed the vote of the town, in its substance and they immediately applied to the Selectmen to call a new meeting on the eighteenth day of February, 1850.

At this meeting few of the petitioners attended, and all endeavors on their part to obtain a calm and fair hearing

were put down by clamor and disorder. It was voted to raise a committee to appear with counsel, at the town's expense, before the Legislature and resist the petition.

Pending the passage of the Bill, the following was printed for distribution : —

THE BILL TO INCORPORATE THE TOWN OF WINCHESTER.

1. This Bill is unanimously reported by the Committee on Towns, after a long trial (eight days), all parties having had more than forty days' notice, the Committee having twice visited the territory; Woburn and Medford having appeared with Counsel and witnesses, and West Cambridge having a representative here to guard her interests.

2. The boundary lines reported are those which the Committee, after actual inspection and full testimony, pronounce the most proper that can be fixed, and which they have stated in the House are so arranged as to work benefit instead of injury to school districts, so as to sever very few estates, and to cross land of trifling value. These lines materially divide but one school district in Woburn, and the inhabitants of that district have declared, by vote, that it could not be so well divided by any other line.

3. The proposed new town will contain two hundred and fifty qualified voters, and the names of two hundred of these voters will be found upon the several petitions asking to be included within its limits.

4. The inhabitants of the proposed new town are nearly unanimous in desiring to be included in its limits. Those now residing in Woburn and wishing to come within the new town, own and represent about five sixths of all the land in that part of Winchester. Less than 500 acres of that land belongs to men who have not petitioned to be so included.

5. The town and people of Woburn are far from unanimous, and by no means earnest in their opposition to the pro-

posed new town. At their Town Meeting, February 7, it was voted by the citizens, and by a large vote, to raise a Committee to agree upon the terms and lines of division. It was not till after large numbers of the Winchester people had gone home, supposing the question was settled, that this vote was reconsidered.

When it was finally voted to employ counsel to resist the petition, the vote was small, and the majority did not exceed twenty. It is a few men, zealous for reasons of their own, and who represent not over five hundred of the eleven hundred voters of Woburn, who desire to prevent the creation of the new town.

6. The printed document circulated by the Woburn Town Committee and entitled "Facts" does not give a reliable statement of the case; it is not candid, ingenuous, or truthful. It magnifies facts deemed adverse to Winchester or favorable to Woburn, while it understates those of an opposite character. Thus it says that the territory of Woburn is "*about*" instead of *over* 11,000 acres. It says that the petitioners take "3,000" instead of *less* than 3,000 acres from Woburn. It says Woburn contains "*about*" instead of *more than* five thousand five hundred inhabitants. It says that the part proposed to be set off contains "*from ten to twelve hundred*" people, instead of *one thousand and twenty-nine*. It says that the "remaining four thousand three hundred to four thousand five hundred are *nearly unanimous* in opposing the separation," when the real number remaining is *over* four thousand five hundred, and when (as we have already shown in Art. 5) there is no reason to suppose that even a bare majority of the whole town is opposed.

It speaks of facts appearing on "the Assessor's Books," as fair statements of the present condition of persons and property, although it was proved to the satisfaction of the Joint Committee that those Books were incorrect when

made, and had become very incorrect by the changes of the
last year; and that many of the petitioners, whom their
" Books" call "*poll tax payers,*" were owners of large
amounts of both real and personal property; in one instance
a citizen worth over $100,000 being put down at a poll tax!

It speaks of the remonstrants as owning 1,374 acres, and
numbering fifty-two, and being, "a majority of them
farmers," when in fact several hundred of these acres are
not in Winchester; when in fact twenty of the so-called
"*remonstrants,*" owning over 700 acres of land, have petitioned to come in; when in fact only twenty-three are farmers, whereas twelve of the fifty-two pay only a poll tax; eight
more own no real estate, and eight more own together less
than nineteen acres of land, — so that these 1,374 acres
dwindle down to less than 500.

It says that the "remonstrants" are "among our most
venerable and respected citizens," although but one man
of all those who remonstrated against coming within our
limits, in case of division, has ever held any Town or State
office whatever — even as Selectman or Justice of the Peace,
so that while the Woburn Town Committee are now willing
to praise, they have heretofore been unwilling to trust, these
their "most venerable" citizens.

It says that the petitioners own but 838 acres — whereas,
those who petition to come within the limits of Winchester
own and represent five sixths of the entire territory.

For the correctness of these statements we refer to the
Committee who reported the Bill.

BENJ. F. THOMPSON,
NATHAN B. JOHNSON,
SAM'L S. RICHARDSON,
OLIVER R. CLARK,
J. A. BOLLES,
FRED. O. PRINCE,

Committee of the petitioners and citizens of " Winchester."

April 20, 1850.

PETITION FOR THE INCORPORATION OF WINCHESTER.

THE following copy of the petition, as well as those of the several remonstrances found here, are in the form of manuscript papers, now in the archives of the Society, preserved by John A. Bolles, and copied by his own hand, — and deposited by him with the town clerk, the originals being in the archives of the State.

The Honorable the Senate and House of Representatives in General Court Assembled : —

We, the undersigned, citizens of the several towns of Woburn, Medford, and West Cambridge, and residing within the limits of the proposed new town hereinafter described, respectfully pray that they may be set off from the said several towns and incorporated into a new town, with the following metes and bounds, namely : —

Beginning at the northeasterly corner, at a stone post on the line of Woburn and Stoneham, near Jesse Dike's house, and thence running along the town line southwesterly about 640 rods to the southeasterly corner of Woburn; thence in precisely the same direction 237 1-2 rods, to a point lying in Medford, forty rods east of Grove Street; thence in a straight line westwardly, crossing Mystic Pond, about 800 rods, to a point in the boundary line of West Cambridge and Lexington, 112 1-2 rods southwesterly from the junction of said line with Woburn; thence northeast along said line 112 1-2 rods to said junction of Woburn, Lexington, and West Cambridge; thence northwest, along Lexington line, about 375 rods, to the southerly side of the road leading from Lexington to Woburn; thence northeast in a straight line crossing the southerly end of Horn Pond, about 820 rods to a point on Main Street, in Woburn, on the southerly side of Pond Street; thence easterly 370 rods to a point 6 rods north of William Richardson's house; thence about 250 rods easterly to the point of beginning, or with such other

limits as may to your honorable body seem proper, and that said new town be known and called by the name of *Winchester.*

Ebenezer S. Parker.
John A. Bolles.
Ebenezer Smith.
Alfred Chapman, Jr.
Leonard Patterson.
David Youngman.
Alvin Taylor.
Solomon Lawrence Fletcher.
Oliver Richardson Clark.
John H. Coates.
Samuel Baker White.
Frederick O. Prince.
William Pratt.
Benjamin F. Thompson.
Nathan Jaquith.
William Matten.
Thomas Collins.
William Masters.
Asa Fletcher.
Ozro Kimball.
Orin W. Gardner.
Samuel B. White, Jr.
Charles Pressey.
L. H. Cunningham.
Warren French.
Hatevil K. Stanton.
Sullivan Cutter.
Abner P. Emerson.
Samuel Stanley Wyman.
Samuel D. Quimby.
Eli Kendall.
John B. Fairfield.
Stephen Cutter.
Stephen Nicholls.
Charles Russell.
Andrew Todd.
Samuel S. Holton.

John G. Usher.
Samuel Kendall.
Joel White.
Charles W. Wilder.
James Adams.
Sumner Richardson.
Joseph Stone.
Nathan B. Johnson.
William W. Shattuck.
Samuel M. Rice.
Joseph Johnson.
William M. Rand.
Andrew N. Shepard.
Austin Buckman.
George Sanderson.
John Buxton.
Samuel S. Porter.
Francis H. Johnson.
Joseph Shattuck.
Salem T. Ward.
James Gibson.
Isaac Shattuck.
Otis Wetherbee.
Phineas Stone.
John Edgcomb.
Calvin L. Parker.
David Woodman.
Josiah Hovey.
Obed Pratt.
Asa S. Kendall.
John W. Swett.
Daniel S. Kingsley.
John G. Hutchinson.
Marshall Symmes, Jr.
Marshall Wyman.
William A. Dodge.
Hiram Andrews.

Charles Kimball.
Edwin Bowman.
George G. Munroe.
James E. Foster.
Edmund Parker.
James E. Abbott.
Henry M. Wyman.
Harrison Parker.
Warren Johnson.
Francis Johnson.
John Symmes.
Joseph B. Symmes.
Horatio Symmes.
John R. Cobb.
Charles McIntire.
Wallace Whitney.
Jonas Woods.
Richard Burnham.
Zachariah Symmes.
Theodore Rogers.
Charles H. Bartlett.
Angus R. Barton.
Gardner Symmes.
Abijah Thompson.
A. H. Hayward.
Joseph Symmes.
Ralph W. Bowker.
John A. Cram.
Roger McNeil.
Patrick Holland.
William G. Chaffee.
William C. Coates.
Benjamin F. Lindsey.
Alvan Cheney.
Robert T. Whitten.
James Bridge.
William A. Warren.
J. C. Emmons.
Allen D. Hunt.
Owen S. Warland.
Moses Hammond.
Joel Whitney.

Lewis H. Priest.
Nathan Jaquith, Jr.
Seth Johnson.
Samuel Whitney.
Henry O. Peabody.
Dennis Harrigan.
G. Stevens.
Stephen R. Ruggles.
R. A. Putnam, Jr.
E. L. Bayley.
David Walton.
William A. Coburn.
Joseph Hill.
Jonathan Clark.
Sylvanus Elliott.
Edmund Tibbitts.
Edward F. Kendall.
Cyrus W. Blood.
Isaac Holmes Kendall.
William Simonds.
John A. Cutter.
Edmund Sanderson.
Samuel Stevens.
Horatio Symmes, Jr.
S. Roberts.
Elmore Johnson.
Horace Hatch.
Josiah Stratton, Jr.
Thomas Warland.
John Whittimore.
Kenellum W. Baker.
Samuel Hutchinson.
Ezra Churchill.
Josiah Walker.
Stephen H. Cutter.
Andrew Cutter.
John B. Lord.
Abner Chapman.
Henry Cutter.
Thomas H. Kaler.
Alfred C. Kimball.
Ira L. Gove.

George Perkins.
Hiram Woodman.
Nathaniel P. Wiggins.
John M. Steele.
Zebadiah Abbott.
John G. Richardson.
Charles Hall.
Isaac P. Wilde.
Samuel S. Richardson.

Matthew Griswold.
Joseph Huse.
Sanford E. Allen.
Samuel C. Grayson.
Retire P. Kimball.
E. N. Pendleton.
Charles Wiswell.
John Vreeland.
Cephas Church.

WINCHESTER BEFORE THE LEGISLATURE, 1850.

It is refreshing in these times, when a petition to our Legislature for the division of a town involves years of struggle and the expenditure of thousands of dollars, to record an instance where the request was granted on its first application and without the expenditure of a dollar for lobby influence or expensive entertainments.

January 19, 1850, a petition was presented to the Massachusetts Legislature, signed by a portion of the inhabitants of Woburn, Medford, and West Cambridge, for a new town to be named Winchester, and a bill was granted and signed by Gov. George N. Briggs, April 30, of the same year.

A short history of this contest — for contest it was — may be interesting to those who love the beautiful town.

After much consideration and many meetings for consultation, the inhabitants of the proposed new town met December 7, 1849; accepted a form of petition to the Legislature, and chose a committee, consisting of Samuel S. Richardson, Oliver R. Clark, and John A. Bowles, to present the same.

The first action of the committee chosen was to visit Woburn, the next morning, December 8, and tender to the Hon. Albert H. Nelson, of Woburn, a retaining fee of fifty dollars and a promise of two hundred dollars additional upon the success of the petition. This proved a wise movement. Mr. Nelson accepted the case, and exerted a powerful

influence upon its result. He had been a member of the Senate the previous year, and knew personally most of the members of both Senate and House soon to meet, and was well and favorably known to them. It was no detriment to Winchester's interests to secure so influential an advocate from Woburn itself. Soon after this date, Mr. Nelson was chosen Attorney-General of Massachusetts, but resigned to accept the Chief Justiceship of the Superior Court.

When the Woburn people found that Mr. Nelson was engaged by the proposed new town they were much disappointed. They immediately chose a committee to oppose the petition, of which committee the Hon. Bowen Buckman and the Hon. Charles Choate were members, both of whom had been members of the Senate, and Mr. Choate was a member-elect for the coming Senate.

Thus the struggle commenced.

A town meeting was held in Woburn, February 7, 1850, at which it was voted that the town was willing the division should be made upon just and equitable terms; but after this vote was passed and many of the citizens of South Woburn had gone home, few members of the meeting remaining, they undertook to reconsider the vote, and a very disorderly scene resulted; but more of this later on.

The work of collecting and placing before the Legislative Committee on Towns all the facts necessary to a favorable result was not small. The *necessity* of a division of the town must be shown; the number of inhabitants ascertained and attested; the wealth of the petitioners and their ability to maintain a town government successfully and economically; also to divide the territory so that no one should be injured in the division; added to this, the preparation of proper bounds and maps for the full understanding of the case by the Legislative Committee, and last, but by no means least, to secure intelligent witnesses who would not be confused in cross-examination and would be perfectly clear in

their statements, — all these matters were to be carefully provided for by the committee of the petitioners, and they had reason to congratulate themselves that their efforts were so successful.

It was of the utmost importance to the success of the proposed new town that the Committee of the Legislature, before whom the petitioners were to appear, should themselves be intelligent and fair-minded, and such were the gentlemen of that committee in 1850.

The chairman on the part of the House was the Hon. Stephen N. Gifford, so well known as the Senate Clerk for the past twenty-seven years. Mr. Gifford represented the town of Duxbury. It was his first year in the Legislature, and it was a mark of unusual confidence that so young a man, new in the Legislature, should be placed at the head of so important a committee. But for us certainly he was the right man in the right place.

· Should the bill be reported favorably and pass the House, its passage in the Senate was considered reasonably sure. The chief labor in the case devolved upon the Chairman of the House Committee.

In the Senate the petition was presented by the Hon. Charles Choate. The town of Woburn made the only active opposition, appearing by counsel in the person of the Hon. B. F. Hallett. Medford and West Cambridge contented themselves with remonstrating on paper.[1] .

A word respecting Mr. Hallett. He was then somewhat advanced in years, and was regarded as the Wheel-Horse of the Democratic party in Massachusetts. Woburn was a Democratic town. Hence, when the Woburn people failed to secure their own townsman, Nelson, as counsel, they did what in their view was the next best thing, and engaged Mr. Hallett; but he was no match in this case for his opponents, Nelson and Bolles.

[1] See Remonstrances, pp. 327–332.

The opening argument by Mr. Bolles was clear, concise, and well delivered, making a favorable impression at once. The counsel on each side appeared to do their best before the committee, and the case excited such interest that some of the meetings were held in the Hall of Representatives.

An amusing episode occurred at one of their latter meetings. The Winchester counsel were contending that Woburn, at its town meeting before referred to as held February 7, 1850, voted its consent to a division of the town upon just and equitable terms. The Woburn counsel contended that, although that consent was first voted, later in the meeting the consent was withdrawn. Mr. Hallett, a "dyed-in-the-wool" Democrat, questioned Deacon Benjamin F. Thompson, who was a "dyed-in-the-wool" Whig, of the Clay and Webster sort, with reference to the testimony the latter had given, "that the later action of the Woburn town meeting was *noisy* and *riotous.*" Mr. Hallett, rising to his feet, most impressively said to Deacon Thompson: "Do you mean to say, Deacon Thompson, that the *Democracy* of *Woburn* in *open town meeting* were *riotous?*" Deacon Thompson paused a moment, then turning to Mr. Hallett in a most polite manner, bowed and made answer: "Your honor *knows more* about *Democracy* than I do." This brought down the audience with a shout of laughter, and Mr. Hallett had no further question upon that point.

The Legislative Committee examined the matter before them carefully and thoroughly; visited the ground, and, after many and prolonged hearings, reported a bill incorporating the new town.

The report, as was expected, was vigorously opposed by many in sympathy with the old towns remonstrating, and as vigorously advocated in favor of the bill. Especially was the argument of Mr. Gifford strong and influential; also that of the Hon. Moses Kimball, then a very much respected member of the Legislature.

The bill passed as it came from the committee and was sent to the Senate, where the opposition was not so sharp, although the Hon. Charles Choate did good work for Woburn. As an opponent, Mr. Choate was a fair and honorable one, and it was thought that his private opinion was not strenuously adverse to the measure. So smooth was its final passage in the Senate that the Hon. Bowen Buckman, the chairman of the Woburn committee, although in the Senate Chamber, failed to notice it.

Though the measure was sharply contested, no hard feelings were engendered; and I think each party, after the passage of the Act, went home with increased respect for each other.

The summing-up by Mr. Nelson, in behalf of Winchester, was masterly in the way of disarming the opposition, and to the opposing parties almost equally convincing.

No money was used by either side to gain influence, not a dollar for lobby or a supper; and when the Legislative Committee visited Winchester, they were given a very plain collation of meats and coffee, with no liquors of any kind. This was in no spirit of parsimony, but the occasion was not felt to require a more luxurious spread; indeed, had the town committee given expensive entertainments it would have injured our cause.

We paid our counsel, Mr. Nelson, two hundred and fifty dollars, and Mr. Bolles, for his legal work, fifty dollars; also paid the necessary expenses of the surveys, printing, transportation of the Legislative Committee, and no other expenses, the town committee making no charge for their various services.

As soon as the bill was signed by Governor Briggs it was taken by the committee to Winchester, and the first day of May, 1850, was a joyful one to the people of the new town. To the writer of this article there never was a brighter or more cheerful spring day; the sun never before shone so

bright, the birds never before sang so sweet, the grass was never so green as on that particular Mayday.

One of the first acts of the new town was to call the petitioners together and assess themselves for the expenses incurred, so as to start clear of debt. Her motto was: "Economy and prompt payment"; and for the first year the leading town officers, as selectmen and school committee, made no charge for their services. Indeed, this was the custom of the school committee of Winchester for the first fourteen years of her existence as a town.

The first school committee was composed of the most highly educated men in town. The chairman was the Rev. John McClary Steele, a graduate of Dartmouth College, and its first scholar of that year. The other members were Mr. Charles Goddard, a college graduate, and the first principal of the Abbott Female Seminary of Andover, and the Hon. Frederick O. Prince, afterward mayor of Boston.

Their first report, written by the chairman, was a model one, and although the town was thus served free of expense, the service was itself of the best.

OLIVER RICHARDSON CLARK.

MAY 14, 1885.

REMONSTRANCE No. 1.

MEDFORD, February, 1850.

THE undersigned citizens of Medford residing within the limits of (Winchester) respectfully remonstrate [against granting the petition of E. S. Parker and others].

John Symmes.	Horatio A. Smith.
Marshall Symmes.	Hosea Dunbar.
John H. Bacon.	Edmund A. Symmes.
S. G. Freeman.	Thomas R. Greenleaf.
Francis Freeman.	

NOTE. — The above is in the form of lawyer's notes rather than an exact copy of the remonstrance as presented to the Legislature; and the sheet, as left by John A. Bolles, Esq., is covered with his comments, through which erasing lines are drawn.

REMONSTRANCE No. 2.

MEDFORD, February, 1850.

THE undersigned legal voters of the town of Medford respectfully remonstrate against granting the prayer of the petition of E. S. Parker *et al.*, to set off part of the town of Medford to a proposed new town.

Peter C. Hall,
Timothy Cotting,
Charles Caldwell,
    Selectmen of Medford.
John Spanell.
M. P. Delano.
James O. Curtis.
John T. White.
Dudley Hall.
Joseph Swan.
Annas Hemphill.
D. Swan.
O. Joyce.
Samuel Lapham.
Joseph Swan, Jr.
Geo. D. Hall.
Geo. T. Goodwin.
Jonas Coburn.
Sanford B. Perry.
Joseph F. Sanborn.
Winthrop Guptill.
D. C. Hall.
Albert H. Butters.
Daniel Lawrence.
Joseph Manning.
A. Blanchard.
A. Blanchard, Jr.
Samuel Train.
J. Howe.
Geo. Hervey.
Joseph Manning, Jr.
John Stetson.
Preston Shepherd.
Luther Angier.

A. F. Sawyer.
John S. Emerson, Jr.
N. W. Wait.
Evan Hall, Jr.
Amos Butters.
Geo. W. Symmes.
E. Lovenow.
Henry Ewell.
S. Blanchard.
Joseph Blanchard.
Joseph Farrar.
E. Davis.
Geo. W. Porter.
John B. Blanchard.
Judah Loring.
Jacob Davis.
Joseph P. Hall.
Gilbert Lincoln.
Elisha Hayden.
John Perry.
George Curtis.
Wm. B. Thomas.
George A. Caldwell.
James M. Sanford.
J. M. Usher.
Jeremiah Gibson.
B. Richardson.
Joseph W. Mitchell.
Joseph N. Gibbs.
Geo. F. Lane.
J. T. Floyd, Jr.
Geo. E. Willis.
H. Blake.
Milton James.

Alexander Gregg.
Joseph H. Vinal, Jr.
Joseph Tufts.
George E. Harrington.
Alex. S. Symmes.
Anthony Waterman.
B. H. Somers.
Elisha Stetson.
George H. Wild.
Thomas Gillard.
J. H. Haskell.
Willard Butters.
James C. Wimeck.
Greenleaf Jauscun.
J. W. Prentiss.

James Hyde.
N. A. Chandler.
W. H. Hastings.
A. P. Hartshorn.
Moses Merrill.
C. E. Merrill.
Ebenezer Teel.
Samuel Teel.
D. H. Hadley.
Stephen Wight.
Isaac Keen.
E. S. Ewell.
Gorham Brooks.
T. R. Raymond.

REMONSTRANCE No. 3.

WEST CAMBRIDGE, February 1, 1850.

THE undersigned *inhabitants* of the town of West Cambridge ask leave to remonstrate against the petition of E. S. Parker and others, for the incorporation of a new town, to be composed of parts of the present towns of Woburn, Medford, and West Cambridge, for the following reasons, namely: —

1. The present town of West Cambridge is small in point of territory, the whole area being only about 4,000 acres.

2. It is symmetrical in its form, being nearly square, and bounded on the northeast and southeast by ponds and a natural stream.

3. The school districts are supposed to be permanently fixed, and to the satisfaction of the present inhabitants.

4. That the territory proposed to be incorporated in a new town was set off to the town of West Cambridge, from the town of Charlestown, in 1842, by the mutual consent and agreement of all parties, — with many other reasons which your remonstrants forbear to mention.

Luke Wyman.
Stephen Symmes.
Joseph Symmes.
Benjamin M. Swan.
George Swan.
Stephen Swan.
Geo. F. Muckler.
James Russell.
Thomas R. Cushing.
W. J. Lane.
Charles Cutter.
Moses Proctor.
Luke Agur.
William Cutting.
Abel Green.
Leonard Spalding.
Martha Gardner.
James Wyman.
Abel Pierce.
Oliver H. Pierce.
Thomas O. Hutchinson.
Thomas Hutchinson.
Clark Brown.
Nathaniel Hill.
James A. Pierce.
James S. Russell.
Daniel Kendall.
Addison Hill.
Jefferson Cutter.
P. F. Dodge.
J. G. Dodge.
David Dodge.
Francis Fry.
Louis V. Stanwood.
A. Shaw.
John B. Perry.
Harrison Hill.
Sewall Parker.
David Clark.
James Webber.
W. P. Locke.
William Prentiss.

Daniel Clark.
Wm. H. Richardson.
Elbridge Farmer.
Elijah Cutter.
William Dickson.
Isaac Hall.
Thomas Hall.
Artemas Locke.
Lorenzo Locke.
Benjamin Locke.
Lewis P. Bartlett.
Thomas H. Teel.
Jesse P. Pattee.
Thomas R. Teel.
David Watson.
John Frost.
Isaiah Jenkins.
Daniel Titus.
Joseph Underwood.
Edward Storer.
James M. Chase.
James C. Blanchard.
J. H. Wood.
Thomas I. Russell.
John Gammell, Jr.
Joseph A. Merrifield.
Annie Cutter.
Thomas Russell.
George C. Russell.
Thurston Boynton.
Thomas Ramsdell.
Moses Cutter.
William Hill.
Enoch D. Pattee.
Josiah H. Russell.
T. K. Hutchinson.
Mark A. Richardson.
John P. Wyman.
John Allen.
Albert Allen.
Abner P. Wyman.
James Russell, 2d.

William T. Wood.   L. Wyman, Jr.
Varnum Frost.   Wm. J. Niles.
Nathaniel Johnson.

Presented in House of Representatives, February 11, by Shepard, of Springfield.

REMONSTRANCE No. 4.

Residents of the Proposed New Town.

THE undersigned inhabitants of the town of Woburn, and residents in that part of said town which E. S. Parker and others have petitioned to be set off and made into a new town, respectfully remonstrate against the granting of said petition : —

Dana Fay.[1]
Edwin C. Woodbury.
Benjamin Eaton.
Geo. M. Wyman.
Thaddeus Parker.
Martin L. Tirrell.
Amos Bulfinch.[2]
Henry Bulfinch.[2]
Ezekiel Johnson.[2]
David W. Johnson.[2]
Levi Johnson.[2]
Robert Minchin.[2]
D. B. Parker.[2]
D. W. Clark.
Thomas Winning.[2]
George F. Pendleton.
Samuel W. Taylor.
Lowell W. Pierce.[1]
Amos E. Cutler.
Jonathan Locke.[1]
Oliver J. Locke.[1]
Varnum G. Locke.
Asa Locke.[1]
Asa Locke, Jr.[1]

Josiah Locke.[1]
D. W. Locke.[1]
Amasa Richardson.[2]
Wm. Adams.
Jacob Pierce. [2]
Gilbert Richardson.
Gerrish R. Richardson.
Charles W. Stevens.
Joseph J. Leighton.
L. H. Allen.
James Thing.
Joel Carter.
Lemuel Richardson.[2]
Peter Valentine.[2]
Thomas S. Fletcher, 2d.[2]
Stillman Fletcher.
Samuel Richardson.[2]
Amasa M. Richardson.[2]
Jonathan Gerry.
Zachariah Richardson, Jr.[2]
Daniel Hadley.[1] [2]
Luther Richardson.[1] [2]
Peleg Lawrence.[1]
Samuel H. Davis.

Samuel H. Davis, Jr.

Jonathan Eaton.[2]

Cyrus Hadley.[2]

Zachariah Richardson.[2]

B. B. Lathe.[2]

Samuel F. Delano.

Presented by Senator Choate, February 15.

Those marked [1] ask to be assigned to Winchester in case of a division.

Those marked [2] are apparently designated by Mr. Bolles as "border men"; some of them living outside of the proposed lines.

BIRTHS REGISTERED IN WINCHESTER, 1850.

DAVID YOUNGMAN, *Registrar.*

June 8, Charles Winchester Coburn.

June 18, Henrietta F. Gidley.

August 13, Frederick M. Symmes.

August 23, Florence M. Kimball.

August 31, Norman Eaton.

September 23, Emma A. Stone.

October 13, Alexander Cameron.

October 17, Charles E. Sanderson.

November 11, Stephen A. Bulfinch.

November 17, Michael Holland.

December 1, Florence M. Eastman.

December 5, Frederick Wright.

December 7, James H. Hatch.

December 12, Daniel H. Hadley.

December 14, Anna E. Hunter.

December 15, Sylvia F. Haywood.

December 16, Josiah F. Stratton.

December 17, Charles W. Blaisdell.

December 23, Frederick Sumner.

GEORGE W. SPURR, *Town Clerk.*

WINCHESTER, June 19, 1885.

MARRIAGES SOLEMNIZED IN WINCHESTER IN 1850. — DAVID YOUNGMAN, *Registrar.*

Date of Marriage.	Names of Groom and Bride.	Age.	Residence.	Occupation.	Place of Birth.	What Marriage.	Name of Parents.	Name and Official Station of the Person by whom Married.
1850.								
May 23.	Lewis Morrill.	22	Winchester.	Shoemaker.	Moultonboro', N.H.	First.	Sewall Morrill.	John M. Steele, Clergyman.
	Sarah E. Dexter.	20	Somerville.		Charlestown.	"	Richard Dexter.	
May 28.	Stephen A. Holt.	29	Milton, Vt.	Clergyman.	Norway, Me.	"	Uriah Holt.	John M. Steele.
	Nancy W. Cutter.	20	Winchester.		South Woburn.	"	Henry Cutter.	
July 4.	Owen S. Warland.	23	Winchester.	Currier.	Portsmouth, N. H.	"	Thos. Warland.	Thomas Streeter, Clergyman, Boston.
	Jane Murphy.	21	Winchester.		Nantucket.	"		
Aug. 24.	Ambrose Fabery.		Winchester.	Laborer.	Germany.	"		Hosea Ballou, 2d, Clergyman, Medford.
	Florian Frethi.		Winchester.		Germany.	"		
Dec. 25.	Fred'k W. Baker.	28	Boston.	Merchant.	Parishville, N. Y.	"	John R. Baker.	B. C. Grafton, Clergyman.
	Mary L. Eaton.	21	Winchester.		Woburn.	"	Timothy Eaton.	

DEATHS REGISTERED IN WINCHESTER IN 1850.

DAVID YOUNGMAN, *Registrar.*

Date.	NAME.	Years.	Months.	Days.
1850.				
May 13.	David Cummings	63	6	10
June 2.	Elizabeth Marsters	94	3	
June 8.	Catherine D. Sharon	1	3	
June 10.	Mary Jane Coates	82	5	20
June 19.	George F. Muckler	25	4	
July 30.	Martha R. Wyman	17	8	
Aug. 21.	Samuel Stevens	32		
Aug. 23.	Samuel H. Davis	48		
Sept. 14.	Marinda Coburn	21	1	
Oct. 16.	Zachariah Symmes	70	9	
Oct. 23.	Joseph Ford	10	7	
Oct. 26.	Elvira E. Cutler	2	9	
Nov. 13.	Anne Buckman	20	7	
Nov. 15.	Henrietta F. Gidley		5	
Dec. 25.	Gardner Symmes	6	3	7

GEORGE W. SPURR, *Town Clerk.*

WINCHESTER, June 19, 1885.

ASSESSORS OF THE TOWN OF WINCHESTER SINCE ITS INCORPORATION.

1850. Cyrus Bancroft, Ezekiel Johnson, Gardner Symmes.

1851. Cyrus Bancroft, Gardner Symmes, Thos. Hutchinson.

1852. Cyrus Bancroft, Marshall Symmes, John S. Richardson.

1853. Cyrus Bancroft, Marshall Symmes, Hiram Andrews.

1854. Cyrus Bancroft, Joshua Lane, Oliver J. Locke.

1855. Cyrus Bancroft, Asa Fletcher, Alvin Taylor.

1856. Cyrus Bancroft, Asa Locke, Jr., Marshall Symmes.

1857. Cyrus Bancroft, Asa Locke, Jr., Marshall Symmes.

1858. Cyrus Bancroft, Marshall Wyman, Samuel M. Rice.

1859. Cyrus Bancroft, Marshall Wyman, Stephen H. Cutter.

1860. Cyrus Bancroft, Marshall Wyman, Horatio Symmes.

1861. Cyrus Bancroft, Marshall Wyman, Stephen H. Cutter.

1862. Cyrus Bancroft, Loring Emerson, Albert Ayer.

1863. Asa Fletcher, Albert Ayer, Loring Emerson.

1864. Loring Emerson, Albert Ayer, Charles Pressey.

1865. Albert Ayer, A. H. Field, Charles Pressey.

1866. Albert Ayer, A. H. Field, Charles Pressey.

1867. Luther Richardson, Josiah F. Stone, Jacob C. Stanton, Jr.

1868. Josiah F. Stone, Asa Fletcher, Jacob C. Stanton, Jr.

1869. Josiah F. Stone, Asa Fletcher, Jacob C. Stanton, Jr.

1870. Josiah F. Stone, Albert Ayer, Jacob C. Stanton, Jr.

1871. Josiah F. Stone, Sumner Richardson, Josiah L. Smith.

1872. William Adams, Albert Ayer, Asa Fletcher.

1873. Albert Ayer, William Adams, Asa Fletcher.

1874. Albert Ayer, Asa Fletcher, Andrew N. Shepard.

1875. Albert Ayer, Josiah F. Stone, William Adams.

1876. Albert Ayer, Asa Fletcher, William Adams.

1877. Albert Ayer, Asa Fletcher, Josiah F. Stone.

1878. Albert Ayer, Asa Fletcher, Josiah F. Stone.

1879. Albert Ayer, Asa Fletcher, Mial Cushman.

1880. Albert Ayer, Charles Pressey, Sherburne F. Sanborn.

1881. Albert Ayer, Mial Cushman, Geo. W. Spurr.
1882. Albert Ayer, Mial Cushman, Geo. W. Spurr.
1883. Albert Ayer, Mial Cushman, Geo. W. Spurr.
1884. Albert Ayer, Geo. W. Spurr, James Russell.

Prepared by ALBERT AYER, *Chairman of Selectmen.*
WINCHESTER, March, 1885.

ITEM FROM FILES OF THE BOARD OF HEALTH.

To the Honorable the Selectmen of the Town of Winchester:—

I would most respectfully represent that there is a nuisance (as I believe) near the Main Street, a short distance north of my house, of a most offensive character, represented to be a manufactory of varnish for what is called patent leather; and carried on by one Mr. Wharf; which manufactory I believe to be injurious to the health as well as very offensive to all who come or are within its influence; and I would most respectfully request your Honorable Board to cause the same to be abated, and as in duty bound will ever pray.

(Signed)   H. K. STANTON.
WINCHESTER, December 16, 1850.

DITTO FROM THE FILES OF THE OVERSEERS OF THE POOR.

PLYMPTON, November 24, 1873.

*Mr. Stanton,—*i Received your leter the 22 October i will say to you that i shall keep the Children if i have to keep them without expense to your town i would like to have you Come here and see the children you might think Beter than to have them Seperated.   Yours with respect
CLERK McPHINREY.

DITTO FROM THE FILES OF THE SELECTMEN.

STONEHAM, August 24, 1874.

To the Celectmen of Winchester,— I Clame my redisdence in Stoneham and I pay my poll tax heare.
JAMES CANNON.

THE WINCHESTER MUTUAL BENEFIT ASSOCIATION.

THE Winchester Mutual Benefit Association was organized March 19, 1883, with the selection of the following-named officers: —

> David N. Skillings, *President.*
> George G. Stratton, *Vice-president.*
> William A. Snow, *Secretary.*
> George F. Hawley, *Treasurer.*

DIRECTORS:

Edward A. Smith.	Henry C. Miller.
Edward T. Wills.	Henry J. Winde.
Sylvanus C. Small.	E. H. Stone.
Henry F. Clark.	L. M. Hall.
Charles H. Cowdery.	

Incorporated under the laws of the State of Massachusetts, April 26, 1883.

Its sole object is life insurance; paying to the nearest relative of a deceased member a sum representing one dollar for each surviving member. Any person, male or female, between the ages of eighteen and fifty, in good health and of good moral character, may become a member upon the recommendation of two members of the association; the admission fee is two dollars; the membership is limited to 1,050.

W. A. SNOW, *Secretary.*

THE SONS OF VETERANS.

THIS association, comprised of sons and grandsons of soldiers and sailors of this town who fought in our late war, was organized on January 14, 1884.

It was voted to name the camp after Admiral H. K. Thatcher, formerly of this town.

At that time the membership of the camp was twenty-

seven ; but it has since been reduced to seventeen, on account of removals from town and various other causes.

The officers for the first year were : —

Charles D. Rooney, *Captain.*
Napoleon Goddu, *First Lieutenant.*
George A. Rooney, *Second Lieutenant.*
John L. Curry, *Orderly Sergeant.*
William A. Snow, Jr., *Quartermaster-Sergeant.*
William F. Edwards, *Sergeant of the Guard.*
William I. Palmer, *Color-Sergeant.*

The officers for the present year (1885) are : —

Charles D. Rooney, *Captain.*
William A. Snow, Jr., *First Lieutenant.*
George A. Rooney, *Second Lieutenant.*
John L. Curry, *Orderly Sergeant.*
Charles H. Rust, *Quartermaster-Sergeant.*
William F. Edwards, *Sergeant of the Guard.*
William I. Palmer, *Color-Sergeant.*

It was voted not to join the National Encampment, Sons of Veterans, until we grow stronger. The company is now provided with uniforms and muskets. The object of this association is to assist the Grand Army of the Republic in keeping green the memories of their dead heroes, and to perpetuate their objects when they are gone.

WILLIAM A. SNOW, JR.

ALL ABOUT THE MILITARY.[1]

IN the War of Independence this town was not behind her neighbors in love of country, nor did she fail to furnish for the general defence a goodly number of gallant spirits, who at the call to arms shouldered their muskets and gave battle to the foreign invader.

The spirit which actuated the old patriots lingers in the

[1] Mostly from the *Woburn Budget*, October 28, 1859.

breasts of their descendants, although with something less of the fire and valor of the early times.

After the Revolution, military enthusiasm continued. The Continental Militia, men unskilled in the arts of war, with rude equipments and ruder arms, had driven from the soil, covered with defeat, the well-disciplined armies of the proudest country of the Old World, and it was natural that the soldiers should be looked upon with pride. To be a soldier was the longing of every boy — to hold a commission the ambition of every man. In the unsettled state of affairs, the people felt by no means assured of their rights, and an organized system of militia was kept up.

This system made it imperative upon every free, able-bodied male citizen to serve from the age of eighteen to forty-five in a military company, and the service so far from being irksome was engaged in with pride by all. All the militia were obliged to parade at stated seasons, for drill and inspection.

In those early times the "Training" was a great event. The privates were expected to keep a gun and twenty-four-ball cartridges always by them in the house, and their accoutrements must be kept in good order. On the morning of the Training Day, the private generally arose before day, — the necessary preparations for service having been previously made, — and, having loaded his gun with a heavy charge, he repaired to the house of his captain and fired it off as near the windows of his sleeping commander as it was convenient to get, and having waked him up, and taken a drink at his expense, the company was ready to muster.

In those days days Neal Dow had not been heard of, and John Hawkins had not discovered the doctrine of total abstinence. Rum was deemed a necessity to soldiering, and had its office at the beginning, in the middle, and at the end of the training.

Many amusing incidents, as well as notable accidents, are

related of these old warriors at militia training. One, whom we will call "Uncle Joe," — not to be too personal in this community, — was of the most patriotic and enthusiastic of "the trainers." On one occasion, having drunk more than his usual number of toasts to Washington, his captain, the ladies, and special as well as general persons and things, his situation the boys took advantage of, and loaded his gun with six heavy charges, putting a piece of "spunk" between each charge and surmounting the whole with a live coal.

The company being dismissed, Uncle Joe started homeward, his gun properly shouldered, and as he jogged, or rather joggled, along, having nearly reached his home, his gun "went off" with a loud report. The veteran was somewhat startled, but concluded that after loading the last time he must have forgotten to fire. As he entered his house he placed his weapon behind the door and sat down to relate to his wife the adventures of the day, including the most singular fact of his gun's going off as it did. While he was speaking of it, bang! went the gun again. This was too much. It might have been a mistake the first time, but this time it must be that the gun was bewitched. The worthy couple were now thoroughly horrified and threw the unholy thing out into the yard, where it lay but a short time before bang! again, the recoil causing it to slide about on the ground in a manner which greatly increased the terror of the old people. And so it continued going off three times more.

Uncle Joe never could be prevailed upon to touch that gun again, because, he said, if it would go off without being loaded, it might, some day, take a notion to shoot him.

The old piece was laid aside till a less superstitious and possibly more abstemious descendant brought it into use.

The militia of Woburn formed two companies, called the East and the West Companies, all persons living east of the

main road from Lowell to Boston training in the East Company, and on the west of that road, in the West Company.

The present sketch relates only to the East Company,— the West Company, the Cavalry Company, the Washington Light Infantry, and the Woburn Mechanic Phalanx to be similarly sketched at another time. Our information, being gathered from various sources, documents, and old citizens, must be in the main correct, and will aid others to recall much pertaining to the older organizations.

THE EAST COMPANY.

Of this company our information reaches no farther back than 1794, at which time Jeduthun Richardson was the captain. Jeduthun was the ancestor of many Richardson families now residing in Winchester, and a very prominent man in all Woburn affairs. His company contained fifty-four members. The captain succeeding him was Jonathan Thompson, under whom we have an account of a detail of two sergeants and twelve men, required by the commander of the regiment, and the age, height, and complexion of each are given, in which it appears that all were of light complexion but two, the oldest forty, the youngest eighteen, the tallest six feet one inch, the shortest five feet four inches. And he reports the numbers of his company as follows: In 1795, fifty-seven; 1796, sixty-four; 1797, sixty-two. On the third of October, 1796, they mustered at Reading; September 26, 1797, at Concord,—to both of which places they marched.

The succeeding captains, from 1797 to 1828, were Joseph Eaton, Bartholomew Richardson, Francis Johnson (under whose command, in 1800, the company was turned out without arms, "to show their respect, at the death of the late Gen. George Washington"), John Wade (during whose captaincy, in 1808, there was a regimental muster on "Wyman's Plain,"—our West Side,—and in 1810 they mus-

tered at Washington), Isaac Richardson, Samuel Tidd (under whose command the regimental order to muster at Wilmington, September 14, 1814, besides enjoining the good condition of their arms and equipments, expresses the hope that ths conduct of the soldiers will be " such as shall do honor to themselves and their country, which, *at this momentous and alarming crisis, demands the greatest exertion* ").

The occasion was indeed momentous, and the " crisis " alarming. The British had just taken Washington; and on this very fourteenth of September, 1814, although Captain Tidd's heroes could not have known it, they were bombarding Fort McHenry, at Baltimore, and Francis Scott Key was detained upon a British ship, whence he watched the stars and stripes flaunting proudly from the fort.

Till midnight on the fourteenth the British guns belched their fury upon the fort, but in the earliest light of the morning they discerned the flag still flying, and he composed the "Star-Spangled Banner," which has ever since been one of our national songs.

" Oh, say, can you see, by the dawn's early light,
   What so proudly we hailed at the twilight's last gleaming,
   Whose broad stripes and bright stars, through the perilous fight.
   O'er the ramparts we watched, were so gallantly streaming —
   And the rockets' red glare, the bombs bursting in air,
   Gave proof through the night that our flag was still there.
   Oh, say, does the star-spangled banner yet wave
   O'er the land of the free, and the home of the brave? "

The redoubtable Tidd, as these associations tend to make him, was succeeded by Capt. John Eames, 1815, whose era was glorified by the following record under date of October 15, 1815: "This day the company appeared remarkably well, every man having on a blue coat faced with red, and behaved to the satisfaction of the officers."

Him succeeded the following list of worthy captains: John Tidd, Stephen Nicholls, Benjamin Wood. Of the latter we have this significant record: —

"Woburn, August 30, 1824. Agreeably to orders, Capt. Benjamin Wood's company turned out and marched to Boston, and were reviewed by General Lafayette." The flattering commendation of the General is not preserved upon the books of the company — undoubtedly a culpable omission. After Wood, came Isaac Huffmaster and William Reed. This brings us down to 1828, and to the last commissioned captain of the Woburn East Company. The membership of the company, during the years included in this sketch, ranged from thirty-eight to seventy-eight, rank and file.

A distaste for the militia organizations began to creep in soon after, and what was once the pride of the people became a ridiculous burlesque with them. Worthless men were elected to office, duties were disregarded, many modes employed to increase the disrepute of the system, and the old militia law became worse than a dead letter.

In 1840 that law was abolished, and thereafter volunteer companies absorbed the military tastes and efforts of the community, and military discipline and tactics were greatly promoted.

WINCHESTER LIGHT GUARD.

Fourth Brigade, Fourth Battalion Light Infantry, Seventh Regiment, Company E.[1]

	Commissioned.	Commission Issued.
F. O. Prince, Capt.	27 March, 1851.	23 May, 1851.
Wallace Whitney, 1st Lieut.	27 March, 1851.	23 May, 1851.
Owen S. Warland, 2d Lieut.	27 March, 1851.	23 May, 1851.
William Pratt, 3d Lieut.	27 March, 1851.	23 May, 1851.
Miran Lawrence, 4th Lieut.	27 March, 1851.	23 May, 1851.
Wallace Whitney, Capt.	24 May, 1853.	4 June, 1853.
John R. Cobb, 1st Lieut.	24 May, 1853.	4 June, 1853.
Oren W. Gardner, 2d Lieut.	21 April, 1852.	6 April, 1853.
William Pratt, 3d Lieut.	27 March, 1851.	23 May, 1851.
Henry Richardson, 4th Lieut.	5 April, 1853.	18 April, 1853.

Officers discharged March 27, 1855.

[1] Roster No. 11, p. 135.

CHURCH OF THE EPIPHANY, WINCHESTER, MASS.

EARLY in the year 1882, through the interest and zealous labors of several ladies, the services of the Protestant Episcopal Church were started in Winchester.

The first service was held in Harmony Hall, on the last Sunday in February (February 26, 1882), the Rev. Charles P. Parker, of Cambridge, officiating. Mr. Parker, although residing in Cambridge and unable to do any pastoral work, continued in charge of the mission services until October 1882, during that time having the assistance of several other clergymen.

The work having been accepted by the Diocesan Board of Missions, the Rev. Charles Morris Addison, Rector of Saint John's Church, Arlington, was appointed missionary in charge, officiating for the first time October 1, 1882.

The attendance having increased by November, the services were held in the Methodist Church, which was hired for Sunday afternoons.

A Sunday-school was organized in December, and early in 1883 the Ladies' Guild was formed. About this time the congregation was organized into a mission, with the following committee: —

The Rev. Charles Morris Addison, Missionary; Mr. Irving S. Palmer, Warden; Mr. Samuel W. McCall, Vestryman; Mr. Frank J. Wills, Clerk; Mr. Charles Gratiot Thompson, Treasurer. Previous to this, Mr. George B. Shepley was Treasurer.

It was soon decided by the congregation that the proper conduct of the services, and the future growth of the Episcopal Church in the town, called for a church-building.

By the beginning of the year 1884 subscriptions were received for a small Episcopal Church, the land on which to place it having been generously offered by Mr. D. Nelson Skillings. Plans were kindly made by Mr. George D. Rand,

and the prospect was so encouraging that work was begun in August, 1884.

The church was completed in January, 1885, and the first service was held in it on January 25.

The church having been fully paid for, it was consecrated by the Right Reverend Benjamin H. Paddock, Bishop of the Diocese, assisted by a large number of the clergy, on Friday, May 29, 1885.

CHARLES MORRIS ADDISON, *Rector.*

WINCHESTER, June 6, 1885.

The following are the names of the members of the Episcopal Church at its formation: —

Charles Gratiot Thompson.
Mrs. Sophie (Underwood) Thompson.
George B. Shepley.
Mrs. Mary Fessenden (Barrows) Shepley.
George Francis Hawley.
Mrs. Harriette N. (Russell) Hawley.
Mrs. Mary Page.
Mrs. Catherine Rice.
Miss Harriet Judkins.
Miss Ellen Judkins.
Miss Mary Judkins.
Mrs. Gertrude Fiske.
Mrs. Susan Boyce.
Mrs. Elizabeth Blank.
Mrs. Mary Delacroix.
Miss Annie Delacroix.
Louis Delacroix.
Mrs. Joseph Moulton.
Henry Bishop.
Samuel W. McCall.
Irving S. Palmer.
Charles Sergeant.

WINCHESTER COUNCIL, No. 150, AMERICAN LEGION OF HONOR.

THE order of the American Legion of Honor was organized in the city of Boston, December 18, 1878, and incorporated under the laws of Massachusetts, March 11, 1879.

At the present time (June, 1885) it numbers over 57,000 members in the United States, and about 6,000 in the State of Massachusetts.

This order differs from the Knights of Honor in three essential particulars. First, it admits both sexes to membership. Second, its benefits are divided into six degrees, or sums, payable at the death of members, namely, $500, $1,000, $2,000, $3,000, $4,000, and $5,000, with amount of assessments to correspond. Third, its assessments are graded according to the age of members at initiation.

Winchester Council No. 150 was instituted in Oma Hall (Richardson's Block), April 7, 1880, by Deputy Supreme Commander Andrew Dow, of Boston, in presence of Grand Commander D. B. Kimball, of Salem, and the Secretary of the Grand Council of Massachusetts. The following sixty-one ladies and gentlemen were present and were initiated and enrolled as charter members, officers installed, and Committees appointed as designated:—

Mr. Abijah Thompson. (Sentry.)
Mrs. Maria Stearns Thompson.
Mr. William Harrison Bailey. (Commander.)
Mrs. Susan Caroline Bailey. (Entertainment Com.)
Mr. George Porter Brown. (Trustee.)
Mr. William Alanson Snow. (Guide.)
Mr. Charles Harrison Dunham. (Trustee.)
Mrs. Mary Elizabeth Dunham. (Entertainment Com.)
Mr. Warren Johnson.
Mr. Henry Childs Miller. (Past Commander.)
Mrs. Mary Hannah Miller. (Entertainment Com.)
Mr. Edwin Augustus Wadleigh. (Vice-commander.)
Mr. Edward Henry Stone.
Mr. Charles Eben Swett. (Orator.)

Mr. James Paschal Boutwell. (Warden.)

Mrs. Hannah Huntington Boutwell.

Mr. John Winslow Richardson.

Mrs. Rebecca Reeves Richardson.

Mr. William Simonds.

Mrs. Mary Roby Simonds.

Mr. Charles Fitch Lunt. (Chaplain.)

Mrs. Sarah Webster Lunt.

Mr. Henry Augustus Emerson. (Collector.)

Mrs. Sarah Emeline Emerson.

Mr. Irving Stevens Palmer. (Treasurer.)

Mrs. Eugenia Elizabeth Palmer.

Mr. Thomas Sinclair Spurr.

Mrs. Fannie Baxter Spurr.

Miss Emma Collamore Richardson. (Entertainment Com.)

Dr. Daniel Webster Wight. (Medical Examiner.)

Mrs. Mary Elizabeth Wight.

Dr. Frederick Winsor. (Medical Examiner.)

Mr. Harrison Parker, 2d.

Mrs. Fannie Fletcher Parker.

Mr. Charles Fernald Jordan.

Mrs. Margaret Louise Jordan.

Mr. James Henry Winn.

Mrs. Julia Ann Winn.

Mrs. Charles Sanborn Smith.

Mrs. Abbie Smith.

Mr. Samuel Wallace Smith.

Mr. Abraham Prescott Palmer.

Mr. Wallace Prescott Palmer.

Mrs. Helen Sarah Palmer.

Mr. Henry Edwin Gardiner Andrews.

Mr. Leonidas Marshall Hall.

Mr. Warren Francis Foster. (Secretary and Trustee.)

Mr. George Washington Blanchard.

Mr. Marcus Carlon Cook.

Mr. George Washington Spurr.

Mr. Erving B. Whitney.

Mr. Sylvanus Cobb Small.

Mr. Henry Stone.

Mr. Benjamin Franklin Holbrook.

Mr. William Henry Cooper.

Mrs. Susan Pond Cooper. (Entertainment Com.)

Mr. Frank M. White.
Mrs. Mary Maria Twombly.
Miss Jennie M. Cummings.
Miss Josephine Keyes.
Mr. William Nelson Arnold.

Several of the above were termed, by the laws of the order, "Honorary members," not being able to pass a satisfactory medical examination to enable them to participate in the life insurance feature of the order. All of these, however, withdrew during the first year or two, after the social exercises began to decline. For the good people of Winchester, like most other communities, lose their enthusiasm for, and become indifferent to, their social institutions as soon as a few leading spirits grow weary of doing all the work of providing entertainments for their fellow-citizens.

The Council now numbers fifty (50) members, — thirty-five male (35) and fifteen female (15), — all "beneficial members," and is one of five councils in the State, of equal age, that has escaped the hand of death, and has consequently drawn nothing from the Relief Fund of the order, while it has paid in over $6,500, and has also paid to its own members in sick-benefits nearly $100, during the first five years of its existence.

The presiding officers have been: —

Past Commander, William H. Bailey (charter), 1880.
Past Commander, Charles E. Swett, 1881–82.
Past Commander, Thomas S. Spurr, 1883–84.
Past Commander, James P. Boutwell, 1885.

The Council now meets on the second and fourth Mondays of every month in apartments of Masonic Hall.

WILLIAM HARRISON BAILEY.

WINCHESTER, June 22, 1885.

AMOS WHITTEMORE.

AMOS WHITTEMORE,[1] the ingenious mechanic and inventor (see p. 126 of *The Record*), was born in Arlington, April 14, 1814, and died in Cambridgeport, July 19, 1882. He was the grandson of Amos Whittemore, the inventor of the celebrated machine for making cotton and wool cards. His father was Amos Whittemore, Jr., and his mother, Mrs. Rebecca (Russell) Whittemore, died in Arlington, Massachusetts, April 5, 1883, aged 97 years, 8 months. His mother was a widow for fifty-five years, — his father dying in the year 1827. His grandfather, the inventor, died in the year 1828.

Amos Whittemore, the grandson, was thus early thrown upon his own resources for a livelihood; but throughout life he was an example of one impelled by hereditary inventive instinct. At the age of eighteen he invented the machine for pegging shoes, mentioned by Mr. Clark on page 126 of *The Record*, as being placed in the mill-building belonging to Mr. Samuel S. Richardson in Winchester. (We are grateful to Mr. Clark for this item of information in his very suggestive articles.) We presume this machine was placed in that factory through the influence of Mr. Whittemore's brother-in-law and ever kind friend, Dr. Benjamin Cutter, of Woburn (my father).

The pegging-machine was an important adjunct to the shoe-manufacturing interest in this country. Mr. Whittemore's plan also embraced machines for cutting the uppers and soles, for buffing and paring the soles and heels, and using wire nails for fastening the heels. The slanting of the pegs in shoes is his idea. His invention was exhibited at Arlington, in December, 1833, but, meeting with discouragement and bitter opposition, was not patented. The machine was eventually sold for forty-five dollars, and others afterward

---

[1] Not Whitt*i*more, as given on page 126, but Whittemore.

reaped the advantages pecuniarily. The true source of the machine has since been recognized, and its utility is generally acknowledged. At an interview with Mr. Whittemore on December 1, 1870, he said that at the time when he invented his machine it was argued that the making of shoes by machinery would throw the shoemakers working by hand out of employment, and it was threatened to burn him out even, if he continued using his machine. Through the influence of his brother-in-law, Dr. Benjamin Cutter, of Woburn, women were induced to bind his shoes, but only at double prices, and this only for a short time.

An obituary notice in the *Arlington Advocate*, for July 29, 1882, by the present writer, contains a list of some of his other inventions. The philanthropic aim of his work in inventing the pegging-machine may be expressed in the words of Mr. Whittemore, when he said, in my hearing: "Many. more people wear shoes than would have worn them had no machines been invented."

His pill-counting machine, for instance, is a good illustration of the quality of his inventive genius. By a contrivance so simple that one feels almost ashamed that he never thought of it himself, a hundred or more pills are counted instantly by a movement of the hand. Mr. Whittemore married, in 1837, Mrs. Almira Thompson, of Woburn, who survives him. They had no children.

W. R. CUTTER.

Woburn, August, 1885.

KNIGHT TEMPLARS' EXCURSION.

AMONG the pleasant excursions of the summer of 1885, none were more so than that of Boston Commandery Knight Templars, on Thursday, September 3, to Star Island. one of the Isles of Shoals. Leaving Boston by a special train at 9.35 A.M., two hundred and twenty-five Sir Knights

and Ladies were swiftly conveyed to Portsmouth, and
there embarked on board the United States steamer
Leyden, which, after ten miles' sail on the water, safely
landed them on the island at 1.20 P.M. They found the
Oceanic Hotel gayly decorated with flags, bunting, Chinese
lanterns, and the words "Welcome, Knights," on an arch
over the entrance of its hospitable doors, while from
the staff on the cupola was displayed a large white beausant
bearing a red Templar cross. Over this was afterward to
be seen the black-and-white beausant of Boston Commandery, which, during the passage on the steamer, had been
displayed at her foremast head. This beausant had been
planted on the summits of Mount Washington and the Sierra
Nevadas in previous pilgrimages.

After removing the dust of travel, the company sat down
to a dinner of excellent quality, well cooked and well
served. After dinner the ladies and gentlemen strolled
around and viewed the many ancient relics which are to be
seen there. Among them were the old stone church, the
original one having been built two hundred years ago and
afterward destroyed by fire, and the present one eighty-five
years before; the monument to Captain John Smith, who,
it is claimed, discovered these isles in 1614, but whose claim
is very much disputed; the "Teacher's Chair," as it is
called, where, in 1848, a Miss Underhill, a loved and valued
teacher, was washed away out to sea, while reading a
book; the little enclosure where some children of the Rev.
Mr. Beebe, a former pastor, are buried. It lies at the base of
several high rocks, and it was laid out and a wooden picket
fence erected around it by the minister's own hands, who
also placed a small monument on the spot. The burial-place
has been sadly neglected of late years, being overgrown with
bushes, and the monument is hardly discernible. The last
resting-places of a large number of the early inhabitants
of the isle are scattered indiscriminately around, and one

cannot walk without treading on the mounds which cover their remains or stumbling over the rough pieces of stone, merely stuck in the ground at the head and foot of the graves. The grave of the Rev. Mr. Tuck, who died in 1701, and that of the Rev. Mr. Stevens, who died in 1740, are more prominently marked by large tablets set upon stone, setting forth their position and their virtues, but the ruthless hand of time has almost obliterated the masonry and the letters. Betty Moody's Cave, said to be marked with the blood of her offspring, whose life she sacrificed rather than have it fall into the hands of the Indians, is pointed out to the curious seeker. The remains of the old fort, built in 1653, on a slight elevation near the hotel, commands a fine view, and is now occupied by a band-stand and a summer-house. While in the neighborhood of the "Teacher's Chair," and also in front of the hotel, the Sir Knights and Ladies were clustered in a group and photographed. After this and during the time of their stay here, most of the company went over to Appledore, in the little steam-launch *Pinafore*, and viewed the hotel — the "Prince of Whales," Mrs. Thaxter's pretty cottage, and the last resting-place of Laighton, the father of the present proprietors of this island.

Returning to Star, and when darkness had settled down on sea and land, the "Oceanic" was illuminated by a large number of Chinese lanterns and a brilliant display of fireworks, given under the direction of Sir B. M. Wedger, lasting an hour. This was followed by dancing in the large hall of the hotel, to the music of Carter's Orchestra, and the closing exercises were the singing of familiar hymns and songs in the same hall, under the leadership of Sir W. F. Miller, until a late hour. After breakfast the next morning, by invitation of the Rev. Sir O. A. Roberts, a goodly number the Knights and Ladies assembled in the old church, where brief religious services were held. After this, by the courtesy of the officers of the United States steamer *Leyden*,

a large number were treated to a beautiful sail around the outside of Star, Appledore, Smutty Nose, Londoner, White, and Duck Islands, while others took smaller craft for the same trip.

At one o'clock the California Pilgrims, who two years ago bore the banner of Boston Commandery to the Pacific shores, celebrated the second anniversary of that event by a sumptuous banquet, to which they invited their less-favored Knights and Ladies. The tables were ornamented with choice flowers and liberally spread with choice and tempting edibles, with as equally refreshing liquids; and the whole affair reflected great credit upon the committee who planned it and the hotel manager, O. F. Frisbee, who carried it out. After the bodily wants had been fully supplied, the large company was called to order by Eminent Sir John L. Stevenson, who, in a few well-chosen words, welcomed all present to this anniversary festival, and introduced Grand Recorder A. F. Chapman, Eminent Commander F. T. Comee, the Rev. Sir O. A. Roberts, the Rev. Sir S. McBurney, of Taunton, and Sir Charles E. Pierce, who made brief speeches. The singing of "Auld Lang Syne," and a general hand-shake all around, brought the festivities to a close, and at four o'clock the company took the boat and cars for home, arriving in Boston at half-past eight o'clock on Friday evening, September 4.

The weather of both days was delightful, and the trip one of unalloyed pleasure to all the participants. Much more might be said about the Isles of Shoals, their history and their attractions, but space will not allow it.

Among those who joined in this excursion were the following Sir Knights and Ladies from Winchester: —

Mr. and Mrs. Charles H. Dunham; Mr. and Mrs. G. S. Littlefield; Mr. and Mrs. J. R. Cobb, Miss Mary L. Cobb; Edwin A. Wadleigh; Mr. and Mrs. James Houston, Misses Ella and Sadie Houston; Mr. and Mrs. G. P. Brown;

Mr. and Mrs. J. F. Dwinell; Mr. and Mrs. F. A. Loring, Miss Bessie Loring; Mr. and Mrs. Abijah Thompson; Mr. and Mrs. W. L. Tuck; Mr. and Mrs. George F. Parker, Misses Mabelle L. Parker and Lizzie A. Symnes; John R. Newman, William Pratt, and George G. Stratton.

E. A. WADLEIGH.

INSCRIPTIONS FROM THE GRAVESTONES IN WILDWOOD CEMETERY, IN WINCHESTER, MASS.

COMMUNICATED BY ABIJAH THOMPSON.

ZACHARIAH SYMMES,

DIED

October 16, 1850,

Aged 70.

" Blessed are those servants whom the Lord,
When he cometh shall find watching."

NANCY,

WIFE OF

ZACHARIAH SYMMES,

DIED

May 21, 1871,

Aged 85.·

" Blessed are they who trust in the Lord."

ASA LOCKE,

DIED JULY 16, 1857,

Aged 75 yrs.

A good man;
Firm and true in friendship;
Faithful in the relations of life;
A follower of the Redeemer.

LUCY W.,

WIFE OF

ASA LOCKE,

DIED DECEMBER 7, 1860,

Aged 81 years.

OUR MOTHER.

Prudent, discreet, and good,
She was an example for her children,
And for many years a helpmate to her husband.
She has now gone to join him in the better land.

CEPHAS CHURCH,

DIED

January 8, 1875,

Aged

65 yrs., 8 mos.

He loved his neighbor as himself.

MARSHALL WYMAN,

July 11, 1792.
July 10, 1868.

SUSAN PARKER,

HIS WIFE,

July 28, 1799.
Nov. 3, 1876.

———WYMAN———

CAPT.

NATHAN JAQUITH,

DIED

Feb. 16, 1875,

Æt. 93 yrs., 10 ms., 16 ds.

We rest together.

MRS. ESTHER,

WIFE OF

NATHAN JAQUITH,

DIED

Dec. 2, 1846,

Æt. 64.

" Whom the Lord loveth he chasteneth."

JESSE RICHARDSON,

Died Dec. 11, 1843,

Æt. 62.

LORA STEVENS,

HIS WIFE,

Died in Winchester,

Aug. 26, 1851.

Æt. 62.

"I go to prepare a place for you."

My parents dear, by faith and prayer,
Sought but their Father's will to know.
And not in vain to them was given,
Through death's dark vale, the light of Heaven.
Yes; there, we trust, with sainted ones,
They sing a Saviour's priceless love,
And there may we when life is o'er,
Meet them redeemed to part no more.

BENJAMIN F. THOMPSON,

DIED

July 31, 1863.

Aged 64 yrs., 6 mos.

HANNAH W.,

WIFE OF

B. F. THOMPSON,

Died Nov. 8, 1882,

Aged 78 yrs., 10 mos.

MAJ. FRANCIS JOHNSON,

Died Nov. 16, 1846,

Æt. 75.

SARAH GARDNER,

DIED

July 20, 1857,

Æt. 85 years, 9 mos.

PATIENCE GARDNER,

DIED

January 23, 1864,

Æt. 90 yrs., 9 months.

JOSEPH HUNNEWELL,

DIED

Sept. 25, 1860.

Age 67 yrs., 5 mos.

CLIPPINGS.

"To-day becomes historic to-morrow."

WOOBURNE.

FOWER or ffive Miles above Mauldon West is a more considerable Towne called Wooburne; they live by ffurnishing the Sea Townes with Provisions as Corne and Flesh, and also they ffurnish the Merchants with such goods to be exported. — *Maverick's Descriptions of New England* (about 1650).

MAVERICK. — Pastor of the "Third Church of Christ gathered at Dorchester, 1631."

DORCHESTER. — "The forme of this Towne is almost like a serpent turning her head to the North-ward; over against Tompson's Island, and the Castle, her body and wings being chiefly built on, are filled (1650) somewhat thick of Houses, onely that one of her Wings is clipt, her Tayle being of such a large extent that shee can hardly draw it after her." — *Wonder-Working Providence,* p. 41.

WINCHESTER (Middlesex Co., 8 m. fr. Boston). — Contains manufactories, machine-shops, tanneries, and extensive vegetable gardens. A branch railway extends to Woburn, a brisk manufacturing place of 10,000 people. — *Taintor's Guide Book,* 1885.

JUNE 2, 1641. — The bounds for Charlestown Village (Woburn) are to be set out by Captain Cooke, Mr. Holliocke and Mr. John Oliver. the contents of four miles square. — *Brooks's History of Medford.*

24. 9. mo 70. A sad accident at Woburn of three men yt were digging a well & ye earth caved in & swallowd up two alive & the third hardly escaped but was digged out his head not being covered wth earth.

4. 12m. 70. Mr. Zacharie Symmes Pastor to the Church at Charlestowne dyed. Fro 19th of 1m. to ye 28th was rainie, stormie & tempestuous weather.

8th 9. m 71. An Indian executed & hung up in chaines for murdering an English maid at Woburn. — *Roxbury Parish Records,* 1670. *Boston Commissioners' Report, 2d Edition.*

SILVER WEDDING.

THE occasion of the Silver Wedding, as it is termed, of Hon. John A. Bolles and wife, was improved by some thirty of their friends who called upon them one evening last week, at their residence, to congratulate them upon reaching this period of their wedded life, and to present to them some substantial token of their regard and esteem. The evening was pleasantly and agreeably passed in social converse and friendly greeting. During the evening Mr. and Mrs. Bolles were presented with numerous articles of silverware by their friends, which were appropriately received. — *Excelsior.*
WINCHESTER, December 3, 1859.

FREEMEN (from Lists in the New Eng. Hist. and Gen. Register) : —

Richard Walker, 1633.
John Walker, 1634.
Augustine Walker. 1641.
Henry Walker, 1672.
Israel Walker, 1674.
Samuel Walker, 1674.
Jno. Walker, 1677.
Joseph Walker, 1678.
Thomas Walker, 1680.

John Walker (1677), John Carter, John Berbene. These psons are in full communion with the Church of Christ in Woburn desireing their fredome. — *Old Records.*

THE story of our division from the three towns is full of interest and excitement. It is a history of conflict and struggle — sharp, earnest, resolute. The warmth of feeling provoked by that controversy is passing away. — *Oration of John A. Bolles, July 4, 1860.*

HUMPHREY B. HOWE.

"A HIGHLY respected citizen of Medford died Sunday, August 30, 1885, aged sixty-seven. He was for many years connected with the firm of Kidder, Peabody & Company, served nine months in the War of the Rebellion and belonged to Post 66, G. A. R." He was formerly a resident of Winchester, and in 1843 was clerk of the old School Ward, No. 5, South Woburn. He also kept, for a time, a grocery-store in the old store built by Mr. John Symmes, which, at a later date, was converted into a dwelling-house, owned and occupied by Mr. Jefferson Ford. (See p. 127 of *The Record.*) Mr. Howe, for a time, also occupied the shoe-factory building of S. S. Richardson (built 1837), keeping there groceries and dry-goods; at one time was postmaster and was highly respected here as well as later at Medford.

WINCHESTER HIGHLANDS.

ANOTHER entertainment has been held, this time in the Congregational vestry, to aid the building fund for a chapel at the Highlands. A company of young ladies, from the Phillips Church, South Boston, kindly came out and rendered, with very pleasing effect, the "Sunflower" chorus. Mr.

Walter Rice gave two solos upon the violin. Mrs. Bailey sang two songs. Mrs. Miller also sang twice. Miss Carrie Pond gave two piano solos, and Miss Mattie Richardson read, with much acceptance, a selection from Mrs. Browning's poems, Mr. Usher making the announcements.

8628. ABOUT THE BALDWIN APPLE (*Boston Transcript*). — I was born in Woburn, and lived there till 1838. I often heard of the apple, through my father, Leonard Thompson, and others.

When Samuel Thompson was surveying, in the fall of 1760, at Butters Row, in Wilmington, Massachusetts, near Woburn, he noticed some excellent fruit on an old apple-tree, inhabited by a family of woodpeckers. He gathered specimens of the fruit, and, finding it very palatable, took some home, where they were much liked, and in after years scions were cut from the tree and sent far and wide. It is now the Baldwin apple of the day.   W. T.

THE WEDGEMERE TENNIS CLUB of Winchester opened its new grounds with a tournament. Ladies and gentlemen attended in large numbers, and the scene was animated and brilliant. The club is firmly established in popular favor in Winchester, and its permanent success seems to be assured beyond a doubt.
JUNE 17, 1885.

HIGH SERVICE.

GROUND has been broken for the high-pressure service (water-works). A large force of men are at work making the necessary pipes, and lining them with cement, for immediate use when all things are in readiness to lay them.
JULY 17, 1885.

STATISTICS.

THE amount of church property exempt from taxation in this town is $76,600. The Assessors report the following figures : —

	1885.
Valuation of Real Estate,	$3,069,722.00
„ Personal „	1,081,355.00
Total,	$4,151,077.00
A gain on Real Estate of	$134,889.00
„ Personal „	264,472.08
Total,	$399,361.08

Rate of taxation on $1,000, $13.50. Number of polls, 1,066, at $2, and 13 at 50 cents; number of houses, 713; barns, 269; shops, 207; dogs, 172; horses, 324; oxen, 6; cows, 186; heifers, 14; swine, 103; sheep, 1; goats, 6; carriages, 248; children between 5 and 15, 620; liable to military duty, 563; women voters, 13.

CENSUS RETURNS. — Population, 1885, 4,390; houses, 713; tenements, 844; families, 857.

THE FORTNIGHTLY.

THE organization of this Association for the year 1885–86 is as follows : —
Mrs. A. B. Winsor, President.
Mrs. Rev. Joshua Coit, Vice-president.
Mrs. George D. Rand, Treasurer.
Miss Sarah M. Nowell, Secretary.

Directors — Mrs. Pressey, Mrs. Seymour, Mrs. Shepley, Mrs. Church, Mrs. Elder, and Miss Harrington.

CHAIRWOMEN OF COMMITTEES:

Literature, Miss A. Harrington.
Education, Mrs. E. Pressey.
Current Events, Mrs. M. F. Shepley.
Social Science, Mrs. A. Church.
Domestic Economy, Mrs. L. Elder.
History and Travel, Mrs. E. B. Seymour.
Art, Mrs. M. L. Coit.
Finance, Mrs. M. J. Rand.

ELIZABETH L. SMITH.

OUR aged townsman, Mr. Samuel Smith, himself an octogenarian, has been called to mourn the loss of his wife, with whom he has passed sixty years of married life, on Sunday last. He receives the earnest sympathies of his friends in his bereavement. Mrs. Smith was the daughter of "Old" Josiah Locke, of Woburn, so called in distinction from later descendants of the same name.
JUNE, 1885.

VILLAGE IMPROVEMENT SOCIETY.

THE Annual Meeting was held September 16, 1885. S. W. Twombly was reëlected President, and Messrs. S. W. Reynolds and S. H. Folsom were elected Vice-presidents.

Executive Committee — D. N. Skillings, John T. Wilson, George S. Littlefield, and Daniel March, Jr.

Secretary, George H. Eustis.
Treasurer, Charles F. Lunt.

250th YEAR-DAY.

SEPTEMBER 15, 1885. Hingham exulted, with bell-ringing, open-air concerts, a great procession, an oration in the *Old Meeting-House* — " the oldest building in the land still occupied for Protestant worship " — by Solomon Lincoln, Esq., more bell-ringing and firing of cannons, a dinner in Agricultural Hall, with post-prandials from the Hon. John D. Long, Governor Robinson, Hon. Thomas Russell, Solomon Lincoln, Esq., Rev. H. Price Collier, Dr. William Everett, and Mr. Luther Stevenson, and a social gathering in the evening, — a grand jubilee over what Hingham has been and done for over two centuries and a half.

PROCEEDINGS.

WINCHESTER. May 5, 1885.

SOCIETY met at Harmony Hall, according to adjournment. Minutes of last meeting read and approved.

The Rev. Leander Thompson, of North Woburn, Mass., and Dr. David Youngman, of Somerville, Mass., were elected Honorary Members.

PAPERS PRESENTED AND FILED.

1. Autograph letter of the Rev. Zachariah Symmes, dated Jamaica, W. I., January, 1706. By Luther R. Symmes.

2. Letters of acknowledgment from the Boston Athenæum, Boston Public Library, Massachusetts Historical Society, Massachusetts State Librarian, New England Historical and Genealogical Society, and the Public Libraries of Woburn and Winchester.

3. Biographical sketch of Dr. David Youngman and his intimate connection with the early history of Winchester. By Abijah Thompson.

4. Catalogue of Youngman's Circulating Library in Winchester, 1854. By A. Thompson.

5. Oration of Abijah Thompson, of Woburn, July 4, 1805. By the Rev. L. Thompson.

6. The Seven Original Members of the First Church. By the Rev. L. Thompson.

7. Woburn Men at Lexington and Concord. By the Rev. L. Thompson.

8. Marriages, Births, Baptisms, and Deaths, 1630 to 1699 (Boston Records). By Wm. W. Whitmore.

Donations were received at, and subsequent to, the May meeting from

The Selectmen, Winchester.
George T. Littlefield, Winchester.
George P. Brown,   ,,

Thomas P. Ayer,   Winchester.
Abijah Thompson,   ,,
William T. Dotton,   ,,
Harry C. Holt,   ,,
Miss Harriet Symmes,   ,,
Stephen Thompson,   ,.
Capt. John Bradford,   ,,
James A. Dupee,   ,,
Joel F. Hanson,   ,.
Henry F. Johnson,   ,,
Charles G. Thompson,   ,.
Edwin A. Wadleigh,   ,,
John P. Walker. Providence, R. I.
Rev. Leander Thompson, North Woburn.
John Ward Dean, New England Hist. and Gen. Society.
George K. Clarke, Newbury, Mass.
Wm. R. Cutter, Woburn.
F. M. Boutwell, Groton, Mass.
Geo. P. Baldwin, Woburn.
Mrs. Albert Thompson, Woburn.
David Youngman, Somerville.
Oliver R. Clark, Tewksbury.
Woburn Public Library.
City of Boston.
Samuel A. Green, Boston.
William H. Whitmore, Boston.
William Boynton, Winchester.
Sumner Richardson,   ,,
George F. Parker,   ,,

The donations of the foregoing included 24 bound volumes. 430 pamphlets and journals, 38 photographs and pictures, 12 historical manuscripts. and several specimens of Indian relics, all of which are duly recorded in the books of our Librarian, or filed in appropriate cases.

A paper was read by George T. Littlefield, containing a list of the original land-owners in Waterfield, included in our present territory, with descriptions of their respective possessions, compiled from the Charlestown Book of Possessions.

The reports of the Librarian and Treasurer were read, accepted, and ordered to be filed.

The following should be added to the list of members heretofore printed: —

George F. Parker.	Edmund Sanderson.
Eugene Tappan.	Sylvanus Cobb Small.
Stephen H. Cutter.	Samuel J. Elder.
Sylvanus Elliott.	Charles Nelson Dodge.
Stephen Abbott Holt.	

Adjourned to meet October 6, 1885.

GEORGE COOKE, *Secretary.*

AN EDITORIAL WORD.

WHILE the title-page of *The Record* simply announces "Printed for the Members of the Winchester Historical and Genealogical Society," it would be false modesty to deny that the wider circle of our fellow - citizens of Winchester has been regarded in this effort to please, instruct, and inspire with local patriotism.

To this wider public we would commend the spirit and intent, if not the manner, of this first volume. It will be considerately remembered that the topics selected from the contributions of the members, or the manner of their treatment, could consistently claim no other merit than that of simple historic information, and even in this, of something less than written history — merely a gathering of material, by any available methods, for the work of a competent historian.

As to the local interest, which it has been the aim of the Society to awaken, we cannot feel it immodest to say that the appeal to the citizens at large requires, at this day, no apology. Not only the families first established upon this soil and such as have left these old homesteads for habitation

elsewhere, but those who have been attracted to Winchester,
— and have as yet to acquire the completed sense of home
with us, — all have a common interest in a "town with a
history."

The day is past, certainly, in the older parts of our country,
when citizens of respectable intelligence will ignore the
historic associations of their homes, or the fact that the
evolution of society around them, to whatever modifications
of thought, faith, or manners it may have brought the living
of to-day, is in the line of legitimate fruitage from the planting of the fathers, — that theirs were the seed-thoughts of
our distinctive civilization; their religious faith the supreme
motive in founding and building, and the Golden Rule the
basis of social organization.

It was a happy inspiration of the lamented Garfield which
led him to say of the dead, on a commemorative occasion :
"They need not us, but forever and forevermore we need
them."

One after another, now in rapid succession, our neighboring towns are celebrating the 250th anniversaries of their
existence. Woburn, the beginnings of which were upon our
soil, was the twenty-third in the order of established towns
in Massachusetts, and the day approaches for the gathering
of what belongs to such a celebration here.

The Society (may we not say the citizens of Winchester?)
is under great obligations to the persons who have so
energetically awakened the dormant interest of many in our
community, and led to earnest efforts in giving a permanent
form to traditionary and fragmentary matters relating to our
local history.

Without special solicitation nearly fifty persons have,
within the year, contributed either written papers or matters
adapted to our archives. Including those not yet printed,
about seventy-five papers have been prepared, many of them
requiring laborious research.

Our acting Librarian, George T. Littlefield, has been occupied in a work which needs only to be known to be very highly appreciated. The arrangement, numbering, and indexing of the matters committed to his care, is a work requiring great ability and intelligent labor. For such work gratuitously rendered, every citizen in time to come will see reason for grateful admiration.

The department of biography has received a few contributions in addition to those already printed, and it is hoped that biographical sketches, or materials for the same, will be furnished by many of our citizens in the near future.

Remembering that it is not official position or professional eminence that constitutes the chief value of a citizen's life to the community in which he lives or to the beneficent structure of society itself, we can hardly estimate too highly the preservation of the material facts of individual and family life.

GEORGE COOKE.

September 25, 1885.

Omission. — The paper upon Roads in Winchester, pages 277-281, should bear the signature of Luther R. Symmes.

CPSIA information can be obtained
at www.ICGtesting.com
Printed in the USA
LVHW020713130222
710998LV00004B/178